...Min slept along-
... with patent med-
... mother's bathtime
... ly done her wifely
... g Jack with a life-
... not sweet but gen-
... meaningful long-term

... y the rabid Catholic
... Jewish banking inter-
... to the international
... in later years - most
... original sin: we are all
... mology was full of tor-
... rienced by saints - most
... eded by visions and rev-

... the young French saint as
... dedicated to her glori-
... published novel, The

... them to friend and
... was only one of a
... His timing was
... fondness for a bet,

... to fire him and make

... spiracy, Leo published
... events, including the
... ated and fanciful family
... some of the etymology
... knight who met 'the great
... were by his unflagging

... he was to form new
... in the cast of char-

... Pete Houde...and
... parochial boundaries

... hand at creative
... The Green Hornet
... ked figure who
... show which fea-

There was no place for cynicism in his young son's worl...
football and track star, good-looking to a sinful deg...
Jack's horizons were expanding through a disparate re...
ing agenda (the poems of Emily Dickinson jostling w...
among others, the wit of wise-cracking columnist Dan...
Runyon and the excitement captured by syndicated N...
York baseball writer Dan Parker), a growing love of mu...
(especially the new white jazz of bandleader Ben...
Goodman, whose drummer, Gene Krupa, was an ea...
Kerouac hero) and girls. Lots of girls, because Jack wa...
good-looking football and track star, even if he w...
painfully shy. Or perhaps because he was shy and not y...
run-of-the-mill cocky, loudmouthed jock.

During his final year at Lowell High Jack met and fell...
love with Mary Carney, a beautiful Irish redhead w...
became special enough to be belle of the close-friends-o...
party thrown to celebrate his seventeenth birthday...
whose attraction was strong enough to haunt him for m...
years. In 1953 he tried to exorcise her ghost by committ...
their fumbling romance (heavy petting but no more, M...
was a good Catholic girl) to the pages of his novel, Mag...
Cassidy, but it only served to rekindle his fond memorie...
the first girl to steal his heart.

A touching and tender account of the anguish experienc...
by every inexperienced young man in love with ...
unreachable - and untouchable - goddess ('Oh lord, wha...
lovelorn Marius I was then!' Jack later confessed to ...
friend, John 'Ian' MacDonald), Maggie Cassidy also de...
masterfully with Kerouac's sporting career, the rigor...
discipline of training, the despair of injury or be...
benched, and the camaraderie... le lock...
room camarad...

No matter how ... arney
most of his life, ... astly d...
ferent worl... had hugely different dreams for ...
future. With Boston College and Columbia University b...

«As to love, who have I ever loved? I am too insane to love anybody else but me, but I have decided to change»

an illustrated biography
david sandison

JACK KEROUAC

First published in the United States in 1999 by
Chicago Review Press, Incorporated,
814 North Franklin Street, Chicago, Illinois 60610
First published in the United Kingdom in 1999 by Hamlyn, an imprint of
Octopus Publishing Group Limited, 2-4 Heron Quays, London E14 4JP

© Octopus Publishing Group Limited 1999

Publishing Director Laura Bamford
Executive Editor Mike Evans
Editors Michelle Pickering, Humaira Husain

Creative Director Keith Martin
Designer Vivek Bhatia

Picture Research Zoë Holtermann
Production Controller Joanna Walker

ISBN 1-55652-358-0

Produced by Toppan Printing Co Ltd
Printed in China

«Between incomprehensible and incoherent sits the madhouse. I am not in the madhouse»

A great many books and articles have been written about Jack Kerouac, and the Net is awash with those who claim some sort of soul-mating with him. I knew him in his prime until his death, from 1947 to 1969, but I am mystified by the increase in his popularity generation after generation since.

Kerouac presents consistent inconsistency, so anyone can have a go. He responded first emotionally to any stimuli, within or without, and he spoke or acted on impulse most of the time. Therefore, it is extremely difficult, if not impossible, to pin him down to any concrete belief or attitude. We do so like to pigeonhole, label and hook people into stereotypes. Books continue to be published that one suspects are written by those more interested in an ego boost or just plain cash rather than any concern for their subject, accuracy or truth, though they may all be partially right.

Fortunately, this one is an exception.

In my dealings with filmmakers, authors or playwrights since Jack's death, the primary distortions come from a lack of understanding or insight into the time in which he lived his formative years – the Thirties and Forties. Society still reflected Victorian values such as "death before dishonor" and Victorian attitudes toward sex. In addition, Kerouac carried inhibitions imposed by Catholicism and his immigrant community, plus attitudes of American Puritanism which were strong in New England.

What many people today do not realise is that Kerouac and his friend and inspiration Neal Cassady were respectful toward everyone, especially their elders and women. They never swore in mixed company, nor was sex ever discussed except alone with a partner or in a group of men. We all took integrity and the bond of one's word for granted. In public, Kerouac behaved "properly"; it was in his writing he could reveal all he felt openly, and true to his feelings at the time. Readers often fail to make this distinction.

Because of his inclination to be so confessional, he revealed his weaknesses, his vulnerability and his hang-ups at the time of writing. He "let it all hang out"; he told it "like it is" – "the TROOTH" – his basic reverence for life itself was a factor largely ignored by later analysts.

In my efforts to understand Kerouac's increasing popularity, I have spoken to dozens of young people in the U.S. and Europe. They can seldom pin down their admiration in words, but one of the words often mentioned is "freedom." Ah, FREEDOM, what has that meant to successive generations? On the surface it appears to have developed since the Sixties into an acceptance of license then chaos, but there is no real freedom without fences. And that sort of "freedom" was not at all what Kerouac intended to transmit. He did not promote free love and drug abuse, yet he has been often held responsible for this sort of license and self-destructive behavior.

He has also been accused of irresponsibility, but people forget that he, himself, had almost no responsibilities in the first place. The only commitment he had was his father's admonition to "take care of your mother." Kerouac took this promise very seriously, yet it allowed for a range of interpretations as to how that was to be done. He did his best. He loved his mother unconditionally and always made her feel good. He accepted her love however it was expressed. She was probably the only person in his life with whom he could be completely himself and unselfconscious, able to do and say anything that came into his mind uncensored by how it would affect

the audience. When he began to receive enough income – and this has been largely exaggerated – he perpetually moved her from house to house, from coast to coast, from North to South and back again – even if it were more his idea of "taking care" of her than her own. He even married a woman he didn't desire in order that his mother be cared for after a stroke. Always, it was essential he be free to move about and find grist for his writing mill. He lived to write, and eventually wrote to live.

He had a carved-in-stone future always in view: when he became too old or satiated with incessant travelling, he saw himself ending up supported by his royalties, living in a comfortable home with a wife and kiddies, debt-free. He would have a private writing room as he had whenever he parked long enough, a cozy fire within and beautiful green and secluded surroundings without, away from the hurly-burly. Nature was an important inspiration, but it would be accessible to the high life of a city. His dream centered on seasons of solitude – he had still to realize how much he needed people.

He expected his dream wife to be not only a perfect traditional wife and mother, cook and household manager but also self-sufficient and undemanding of him – able to entertain herself with hobbies, one of them reading. She would be fun-loving, a bit daring, even "crazy" at times. She would be available to him when he wished to exchange ideas, warm companionship or bodily fluids. He would enjoy the company of the

children for short periods, and he had firm opinions on how they should be raised, with both parents' roles clearly defined. This trait is a clue to why he could not face his daughter, Jan. He wasn't ready to be the "perfect father," so better to pretend that she wasn't his and so relieve him of that monumental obligation. He would expect the mother to handle matters of discipline – he would have been as hopeless as Cassady in inflicting any restraints that might make the child unhappy or momentarily against him. And I doubt he ever got as far as considering the independent bent of a teenager's mind.

Until such time as this scenario might come into being he would not sacrifice his freedom. He did project the dream onto the women he loved, hastily marrying two of them in his impatience to realize his ideals – one through circumstantial pressure, the other on typical impulse. In those days support of a wife and family required a "steady" job; Jack managed to work at a variety of occupations briefly, preferring the relatively unstructured work as a seaman or brakeman, but even that "steady" work trapped him in a cage of time and place and was not sustained.

Kerouac's need for freedom was unalterably melded wih his need to write. He was able to paint such vivid word-pictures of his footloose, responsibility-free life, those who read his works assume he was advocating rebellion from any form of constraint. Many followers have simply abandoned their own responsibilities to school, home, family or society in an effort to discover and enjoy the pleasures they imagine he did – ignoring the suffering he bore that resulted from the Catholic indoctrination that all sensory pleasure was sin. He conjured up the Garden of Eden, but that snake was forever on his back.

I've never heard of anyone able to emulate his experiences in quite the same way. The "beatniks" got it wrong; the "hippies" and the "flower-love children" got it wrong; the mind-controlling "religious" cults got it wrong; and various degrees of "rebellion" have given us poetry and art of dubious merit, drug problems, selfish nearsighted parents and directionless, often homeless, young people. Obviously, Kerouac is not to blame for these developments in society after his time, but a chain was forged resulting from misguided attempts at following him and his contemporaries with a commonplace attitude that any problem one faces is due to some outside event or influence; we ourselves are never to blame, and the vast and powerful inner resources within each of us are ignored and diminished.

Kerouac certainly had no intention of triggering such attitudes. He was in fact shocked by accusations to this effect, so much so that he resolved to drink himself to death. This was the only one of all his myriad plans that he actually was able to fulfill. Personally, I believe that the universal appeal of *On the Road* was his ability to express in such authentic detail his joyful celebration of life on so many levels that it can't help but lift our spirits. He was not so much interested in what is wrong with the world but what is good about it. Kerouac becomes a part of every reader and researcher as the varied interpretations of his life and work penetrate the inquiring mind, to be reinterpreted further according to the selective biases of new readers. Who was the real Jack Kerouac? Who can tell? He offers a kaleidoscope of choices, especially to those who weren't with him in his own time.

Carolyn Cassady

1 **1922-1941**

MASSACHUSETTS TO MANHATTAN

Charles Dickens liked what he saw of Lowell when he visited the city in 1842. It was the eminent English author's first visit to America, and the industrial revolution that had completely transformed Britain was changing the face of its former colony in similar fashion. A noted social commentator and reformer, Dickens was keen to see how the new breed of American industrialists were setting about their task and Lowell, which was the brightest jewel in the American textile-manufacturing crown, was as good as a place to start as any.

above 'Spindle City' – Lowell's mills on the Merrimack's banks at the turn of the century.

right the carnage left in Centerville by the 1936 flood. His print shop uninsured, Leo Kerouac lost his business.

Lying at the junction of the Merrimack and Concord rivers some 25 miles northwest of Boston, Lowell was established by white settlers in 1653, when it was a farming community known as East Chelmsford. At the beginning of the 19th century the abundance of free water power from the 35-feet high Pawtucket Falls and the completion of the Middlesex Canal to Boston made the location ideal for entrepreneurs in the cloth and shoe-manufacturing trades. By 1824 the town boasted a network of canals to serve the mills that lined the Merrimack and two years later East Chelmsford became an historical footnote when the now-thriving community was incorporated as a town and named for Francis Cabot Lowell, a pioneer textile magnate. Ten years later it achieved the status of city, sharing with Cambridge the distinction of being co-seat of Middlesex County.

Dickens wrote admiringly of Lowell's clean, wide and tree-lined avenues, so contrasting with the mean, narrow, grime-encrusted streets that typified Britain's industrial cities. He also remarked warmly about the cheery demeanour and good deportment of the female loom-hands he encountered, and of the $2 a week they could earn as workers in this exciting and dynamic new enterprise. The harsh truth, however, was that many of those loom-hands were destined for early graves, their lungs destroyed by the raw lint that flew about their workplaces, while their homes were mostly ill-built woodframe houses that offered no real protection against the bitter cold of long New England winters.

During the next 100 years Lowell continued to grow apace. While it rose to become one of America's most important industrial sites, earning itself the nickname 'Spindle City', competition from cheaper imported fabrics and rejuvenated post-Civil War southern cotton-growing states began to erode its prosperity; mill owners cut wages and workers began to move elsewhere for better-paid employment. And so it was that Lowell began to welcome large numbers of outsiders who were ready to take on any work, no matter how poorly paid. Immigrants arrived from Greece, Poland, Ireland and French-speaking Quebec, the Canadian province that lay less than 200 miles north and many of whose citizens had long since migrated south to live in neighbouring New Hampshire and Vermont.

By the end of World War I, Lowell – now boasting a population of more than 80,000 – was a cosmopolitan and multicultural city. Each immigrant

group formed its own self-contained community, preserving its mother-tongue and traditions in homes, schools, churches, restaurants and clubs; celebrating its own ages-old anniversaries and festivals; observing its own social mores to create a sense of continuity and stability in a world that had grown increasingly unstable, this being nowhere more apparent than in the field of employment.

Ten years before the first chill blasts of recession signalled the arrival of the 1930s Depression, Lowell began a decline every bit as cataclysmic. One by one the cotton mills were shut down, with the surviving few forced to offer 'breadline' paypackets.

While the rest of America and the developed world began the process of rebuilding from the ashes of the Great War during the fun-filled Roaring Twenties, Lowell's fortunes took a dive. To misquote Charles Dickens himself, Lowell experienced the worst of times amid the best of times.

Jean-Louis Lebris de Kerouac – the name given on his birth certificate – was born into this depressing scenario on March 12, 1922, the third child of Joseph Alcide Leo Kirouack (sic) and his wife, Gabrielle Ange L'Evesque. Their two older children were Gerard, who was five when his baby brother arrived, and Caroline, a sparky three-year-old already and forever to be known to her family by the pet-name 'Nin'. Jack Kerouac himself was to become known to his family as 'ti Jean', little Jean.

Kerouac's parents had met and married in Nashua, New Hampshire, which was some 12 miles north of Lowell, where Leo's father, Jean-Baptist Kirouack, owned a lumber business successful enough for him to send his son to a private school in Rhode Island. Initially spelling his surname Kérouack, Leo began his working life as a typesetter and reporter for Nashua's French language newspaper, *L'Impartial*. His industry and aptitude were to convince its owner, one Louis Biron, to send Leo to Lowell when he acquired the struggling *L'Etoile*, charging the young man with the combined roles of news reporter, advertisment salesman and copywriter, English-to-French translator and typesetter.

Leo was 26 years old when he returned to Nashua to court and marry Gabrielle L'Evesque in 1915. Born in St-Pacme, Quebec, some five miles from the St Lawrence River shore and 60 miles east of the city of Quebec itself, Gabrielle boasted ancestors from Normandy (Leo's were from Britanny), with the exotica of a half-Iroquois grandmother. Her parents had migrated to Nashua when she was an infant, her mother dying tragically young and her father – a mill worker who became a tavern-keeper – raising her with help from his second wife until his own untimely death in 1909, when Gabrielle was just 14 years old. A shoe factory worker until her marriage, Gabrielle would return to that job time and again for much of her adult life, even after her youngest son was a grown man.

There was much more than a six-year gap between Leo and Gabrielle's ages to make them badly mismatched. While Leo's childhood, expensive education and fluency in English enabled him to move gregariously across Lowell's cultural divides, his wife preferred to conduct her life inside 'Little Canada', the city district of Pawtucketville. She was most comfortable speaking joual, the French-Canadian dialect that would be her son's only means of verbal expression until he began his primary education. In fact, Jack would not express himself really confidently in English until he was to reach his late teens.

A devout Catholic, Gabrielle had more reason than most to call on mother church – and the nuns who ran the local St Louis de France Parochial School – for spiritual help and sustenance during the first four years of her youngest child's life. Gerard, her first-born and undisputed darling, was victim to a succession of illnesses that left him without the physical strength to fight the recurring bouts of rheumatic fever that eventually claimed his life in 1926, when he was only nine years old, his wasted body unable to struggle on.

above right Jack's birthplace, at 9 Lupine Avenue – home for Leo, Gabrielle, Gerard, Caroline and "ti Jean."

right shoring up a mill's foundations during the '36 flood.

RIS DE KEROUAC

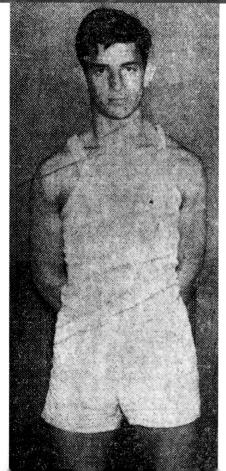

Jack Kerouac's years of infancy were spent in a remorseless and unremitting saga of sickbeds, weeping, woe and despair, combined with the most morbid religiosity born out of the holy sisters' conviction that Gerard was a sainted martyr in the making. It was a conviction that Gabrielle was only too ready to share. Certainly, Gerard was a sincere Catholic boy who had fervently embraced the church's teachings and would preach them relentlessly to his younger brother.

Too young to comprehend, Jack nevertheless received a mass of powerful images, not least of the huge glass caskets that stood like so many spectral sentinels in the grounds of the Franco-American Orphanage on Pawtucket Street. Each contained a garishly painted tableau depicting one of the Stations of the Cross, the 12 stages of brutal horrors inflicted on Jesus Christ on his way to death by crucifixion. Gerard liked to take 'ti Jean' there, talking him through Christ's ordeal in awful detail and leaving the young boy with an emotional scarring that would never heal.

While Jack Kerouac's best-known and most successful novel, On the Road, deals magnificently with the lives of those he knew best during a relatively brief period of his adulthood, much more of his working life was devoted to creating a mass of literature dedicated to his Lowell childhood.

left Jack's more physical talents began to flower in his early teens. By the time he entered Lowell High he'd become a sprint champion and football star.

His fixation with the saintly Gerard—the dead boy his mother would mourn for the rest of her life and against whose perfection Jack was forever being compared and found wanting—would reach its apogee in 1963 with the publication of *Visions of Gerard*. This haunting memoir, first begun in 1956, saw the creation of a key element in what its author called *The Legend of Duluoz*—the fictional name he gave his family in those chronicles.

While Jack was apparently content, for the most part, to go along with the party line where Gerard was concerned ("the strangest, most angelic gentle child," he told his friend, boon companion and inspiration, Neal Cassady, in a 1950 letter), he would forever nurse a guilt-ridden resentment against a sibling he knew to be as flawed as any. A few days before he died, Gerard—enraged when "ti Jean" disturbed something he was working on—slapped the four-year-old violently across the face.

It was a genuinely traumatic episode that Jack recalled vividly in that same letter to Neal Cassady 24 years later, just as he had five years earlier in a letter to his sister, Caroline, during a difficult period when he was undergoing psychoanalysis. It had been suggested that Gerard's slap had resulted in a natural childish wish that the perpetrator would die—a wish that had been unwittingly granted soon after. **"So I felt that I had killed him,"** Jack explained to Nin, **"and ever since, mortified beyond repair, warped in my personality and will, I have been subconsciously punishing myself and failing at everything."**

The real responsibility for any warping of Jack's personality can be laid firmly on Gabrielle Kerouac, however. With her beloved Gerard dead, she turned the full suffocating weight of her overweaning and claustrophobic love on Jack. For some years Jack and Nin slept alongside their mother in the big bed she ought to have shared with her husband. Any sign of a sniffle and Jack would be kept back from school and dosed with patent medicines. Gabrielle also insisted on supervising Jack's most personal ablutions until he reached puberty, and he was a hefty 12-year-old when his mother's bathtime scrubbing caused him to have an erection. Memories of his mother's outrage and his shame would haunt him for years.

Gabrielle considered sex both disgusting and sinful. It was a certitude she would pass on to her son, leaving Jack with a lifelong sense of guilt about his own libido—**"But there's an awful paranoiac element sometimes in orgasm that suddenly releases not sweet but genteel sympathy but some token venom that splits up in the body,"** he later wrote in *Big Sur*. He became unwilling—or unable—to form or maintain meaningful, long-term physical relationships.

Gabrielle was also viciously anti-semitic (hadn't "they" conspired to kill the Lord Jesus?), and subscribed to the core message delivered every week by the rabid Catholic priest, Father Charles Coughlin, on one of America's most influential networked radio shows through the 1930s. According to Coughlin, Jewish banking interests had caused the Wall Street Crash and the Depression, and almost every other social ill could be traced either to Jews or those who had bought into the international Jewish "conspiracy." This, too, was a message Jack Kerouac would absorb and retain, even though many of his most trusted and loyal friends in later years—most notably the poet, Allen Ginsberg—were Jewish.

The nuns of St. Louis de France did their own damage, drumming into Jack the Catholic concept of original sin: we are all born with the inherited guilt of Adam's challenge to God by eating the forbidden fruit. And the forbidden fruit was, of course, sex. The nuns' cosmology was full of tortured martyrs, graphic examples of the horrible suffering endured by those who would not renounce their faith, and the "beautiful" deaths experienced by saints. A particular favorite was the young French consumptive, Thérèse of Lisieux, whose death in 1897, in the Carmelite convent she had joined at age 15, was preceded by visions and revelations she recorded in a diary which became a best-seller when it was posthumously published a year or two later.

Thérèse had been canonized in 1925 and became the focus for a cult-like following whose blind devotion the young Jack would share. He took the young French saint as his own patron and inspiration, even when later sophistication led him to scoff at the kitsch art (replete with cute lambs, roses and fluffy clouds) dedicated to her glorification. It is no coincidence that Jack gave Thérèse's surname, Martin, to the family at the heart of his first published novel, *The Town and the City*.

Jack transferred to St. Joseph's School and the strictures of Jesuit teachers (**"great big black angels with huge fluttering wings,"** he characterized them to friend and biographer Charles E. Jarvis, adding: **"I was at first shit scared of them"**) when his own family moved to Lowell's Pawtucketville district in 1932. It was only one of a number of relocations inflicted on Gabrielle by her husband's ever-fluctuating fortunes.

left St. Joseph's School, where Jesuit "great black angels" took Jack under their wings.

below left High school football star: "You could hit him and he'd bounce right back."

Leo had quit his newspaper job to strike out as a jobbing printer. His timing was lamentable amid growing signs of worldwide recession, as was his decline into drinking when times grew hard. That, combined with Leo's fondness for gambling, was enough to make his family's finances precarious. Even when he found occasional jobs with established firms, Leo's tendency to opinionated plain-speaking would force employers to fire him, and make him few real friends.

Convinced that Lowell's city fathers—council officials, church leaders and factory owners included—were embroiled in a cosy self-serving conspiracy, Leo published his own newsletter, *Spotlight*, to rail against perceived injustices. *Spotlight* also featured Leo's own reviews of theatrical productions and sports events, including the wrestling and boxing fights he occasionally promoted. It barely covered its production costs.

It was Leo who filled Jack's head with a convoluted and fanciful family history that had the Kerouacs descended from Irish Celts who migrated to Brittany via Wales and Cornwall before settling in Canada. While some of the etymology Jack used to qualify his later ramblings was fairly sound (if jumbled), his claims to have recovered memories of a past life as a young Cornish knight who met "the great monsters of Brittany" were inspired as much by the large quantities of alcohol he was consuming towards the end of his life as by his unflagging romanticism and love of the dramatic.

Jack's move to Bartlett Junior High School was to prove a watershed in his life. For the first time, all his lessons were conducted in English and he was to form new friendships that would dominate not only his teenage years but create a network of loyal allies he would rely on for the rest of his life, not least in the cast of characters that peopled the fictionalized recollections of his Lowell childhood.

Principal among them were Henry "Scotty" Beaulieu, Roland Salvas, George "G.J." Apostolos,

Duke Chiungos, Vinny Bergerac, the brothers Mike and Pete Houde . . . and Sebastian "Sammy"

Sampas. Sammy became Jack's soulmate, as together they discovered art and literature, politics

and the world outside Lowell's parochial boundaries through insatiable reading and tireless

discussions that reached remarkably precocious heights.

It was the Houde brothers who turned Jack on to the first English-language "literature" that would fire his imagination and inspire him to try his hand at creative writing—the lurid pulp fiction of detective and thriller comic books featuring characters such as Operator #5 ("America's Secret Service Ace"), The Green Hornet and Phantom Detective. The character who grabbed Jack's attention—and would form the template for his own Doctor Sax, the mysterious black-cloaked figure who prowled the shadows of Lowell's alleys and riverside woods—was The Shadow, the brilliant creation of author Walter Gibson and the star of an eponymous weekly radio show, which featured the distinctive menacing tones of Orson Welles playing the title role between 1937 and 1939.

Launched into print in 1931 to protect the copyright of a character initially employed only to plug forthcoming issues of *Detective Story* magazine, *The Shadow* caught the imagination of America's vast radio audience. It became a twice-monthly novel-length publication in which crimebuster Lamont Cranston ("The Shadow"), dressed in black from head to toe and sporting a pair of deadly 45s, did battle with a veritable army of super-villains, his triumphant peals of mocking laughter signifying another victory over the dark forces of evil.

It was glorious purple-prose hokum, but *The Shadow* (which Jack collected and read voraciously) gave him the spur to create his own comic-book fictions. He became The Black Thief, a character who haunted the backyards of his neighborhood, resplendent in his sister's red and black rubber beach-cape and a battered old fedora, leaving scary notes in place of the toys he would steal from (and later return to) his friends.

Sebastian Sampas steered Jack away from such childish pursuits when he suggested that Kerouac join the discussion groups organized by their school librarian, Miss Mansfield, an inspiration to gifted students whom she encouraged to take their education as far as possible. Miss Mansfield's group would eventually evolve into The Young Prometheans, a formidable debating hothouse in which Jack and Sebastian's budding artistic talents and political ideals would flourish, blossom and bloom.

Sports star Jack's more physical talents began to flower in his early teens. Well-built, strong and muscular, he played baseball with his friends in local parks and was taken up by the high school football coach as a hot prospect when his explosive pace, combined with superior body strength and bravado, made him a formidable running halfback. As Duke Chiungos, a Lowell High teammate during the 1936-38 seasons, remembers, Jack was **"a real tough boy. . . you could hit him and he'd bounce right back."**

Resilience was not a quality Jack's father shared with his exuberant son. In 1936 the Merrimack flooded into Lowell when heavy rains swelled the river and a mass of debris, including telegraph poles from a factory up-river, smashed its way through Centralville. It was a drama Jack would recall with startling clarity and to great effect 16 years later in *Doctor Sax*, proving that nothing escaped his immaculate eye for detail or his remarkable, near-photographic memory. As the floodwaters engulfed whole areas of the town, Leo's uninsured print shop on Bridge Street was irreparably damaged and his business lost. Once more Leo sought refuge at the Social Club and comfort in the view through the bottom of a glass, his faith in the American dream

above and above left remembrance of past glories. Justifiably proud of his early sporting exploits, Jack looks back at his Horace Mann and Columbia clippings.

irretrievably abandoned, his cynicism justified by this latest fateful blow.

But there was no place for cynicism in his young son's world. A football and track star, good-looking to a sinful degree, Jack's horizons were quickly expanding through a disparate reading agenda (the poems of Emily Dickinson jostling with, among others, the wit of wise-cracking columnist Damon Runyon and the excitement captured by syndicated New York baseball writer Dan Parker), a growing love of music (especially the new white jazz of bandleader Benny Goodman, whose drummer, Gene Krupa, was an early Kerouac hero) and girls. Lots of girls, even if the object of their admiration was painfully shy.

During his final year at Lowell High, Jack met and fell in love with Mary Carney, a beautiful Irish redhead who became special enough to be belle of the close-friends-only party thrown to celebrate his 17th birthday and whose attraction was strong enough to haunt him for many years. In 1953 he tried to exorcize her ghost by committing their fumbling romance (heavy petting but no more; Mary was a good Catholic girl) to the pages of his novel, *Maggie Cassidy*, but it only served to rekindle his fond memories of the first girl to steal his heart.

A touching and tender account of the anguish experienced by every inexperienced young man in love with an unreachable—and untouchable— goddess (**"Oh lord, what a lovelorn Marius I was then!"** Jack later confessed to his friend, John "Ian" MacDonald), *Maggie Cassidy* also dealt masterfully with Kerouac's sporting career, the rigorous discipline of training, the despair of injury or being benched, and the jostling, joshing world of all-male locker-room camaraderie.

No matter how much Jack would idealize Mary Carney for most of his life, the simple fact was that they occupied vastly divergent worlds and had hugely different dreams for the future. With Boston College and Columbia University both offering Jack football scholarships, and his own burgeoning ambition to become a professional writer, it was becoming a dead certainty that he would leave the provincial straight jacket of Lowell. However, Mary made it plain that home was where her heart lay, with marriage and child-rearing her only declared goals.

Mary's refusal to go "all the way" led Jack to embark on a secret relationship with the more compliant Peggy Coffey, a feisty and bubbly Lowell High contemporary who was in every way Mary's opposite. That alone doomed their affair, for this would-be singing star's personality overwhelmed Jack's at every turn, though they remained good friends and dated occasionally in later years when Jack returned to Lowell. However, it says much for the hold Mary Carney had on him that Jack would continue to indulge in "what-if" musings about her, even after Mary had married twice and he himself three times.

Marriage—to the big, bumbling but benign and much older figure of Charlie Morrisette—had taken Jack's sister Nin away from home in May 1937, the moment she turned 18 and her mother's misgivings had no legal force. As Jack mulled over his college options, deciding to reject Boston College (only a few miles away) and accept Columbia University (in the heart of New York City, and who knew what thrills lay ahead there), Gabrielle Kerouac steeled herself to the impending loss of her beloved boy.

CARNEY

above the steps in front of Low Library, Columbia University, in the early 1940s.

Money being as tight as ever, and determined that her son should be chaperoned as closely as possible, Gabrielle arranged for Jack to live with her stepmother in Brooklyn, even though that meant a 20-mile, two-hour daily journey through Manhattan to the Horace Mann School for Boys, one of two elite private academies that acted as preparatory schools for Columbia University. Situated in the Bronx's posh Riverdale suburb, Horace Mann's ivy-clad building stood amid manicured lawns on a bluff overlooking the Hudson River with views of the New Jersey shore to the west and the plush acres of Van Cortland Park to the east.

It was a world away from Lowell, not least because most of the students with whom Jack found himself sharing classrooms and gymnasium workouts were quite unlike anyone he'd ever met before. For one, they were invariably rich kids from the Upper West Side of Manhattan. Also, almost to a man, they were Jewish—a tribe of whom he had heard nothing good in all his 17 years. He was quickly to learn that they were just like any tribe, with the same human strengths and weaknesses, as well as the same capacity to offer and accept friendship with grace and generosity.

Chief among those who took to the impoverished, ill-dressed, earnest young newcomer and made his initial entry into their world so easy were Pete Gordon and Bob Olsted, Dixieland jazz buffs whose guided tours around New York clubs were rewarded with invitations to spend Thanksgiving in Lowell. For his part, Eddy Gilbert opened Jack's eyes to an unimagined lifestyle when he invited him to spend weekends at his family's mansion in Flushing. He also helped swell the Kerouac coffers with $2 backhanders for English essays.

But the two friendships that would outlast Jack's year at Horace Mann were those he shared with Seymour Wyse and Henri Cru. The former was a London-born modern jazz fan who introduced Jack to the joys of gigs at places such as the Harlem Apollo, the Golden Gate Club and the Savoy Ballroom. The latter came from a wealthy Massachusetts family of French lineage and was destined to introduce Jack to Frankie Edith Parker, the first Mrs. Jack Kerouac. Cru would be featured under the aliases of "Remi Boncoeur" in *On the Road* and "Deni Bleu" in *Lonesome Traveler*, *Vanity of Duluoz*, *Desolation Angels* and *Visions of Cody*.

Wyse, who would appear as "Lionel Smart" in *Vanity of Duluoz*, *Maggie Cassidy* and *Visions of Cody*, turned Jack on to the avant-garde brilliance of sax players Lester Young (then a member of the Count Basie Orchestra) and Charlie Parker, whose experimental phrasing—flurries of notes building to a declarative crescendo—would later inspire the young writer to attempt the same thing with words, the "spontaneous bop-prosody" Allen Ginsberg called his distinctive writing style. But it was Lester Young whom Jack rated above all, basking in the small glory of having predicted great things for the tenor virtuoso long before he moved from big band horn sections to great solo stardom.

Through another Horace Mann contemporary, Albert "Al" Avakian, Jack also became a regular at Nick's, a club owned by Al's older brother, George, who would go on to become a leading record producer and writer whose long-term friendship Jack valued highly.

Jack's new-found enthusiasm for modern jazz was captured in articles he wrote for *The Horace Mann Record*. This was remarkable, for his presence at the school was ostensibly in the role of a "ringer." Ringers were the dozen or so sporting prospects given scholarships to lend the football team some respectability, and "crammed" to make up academic credits that would justify their moving on to sports stardom at Columbia. Ringers were certainly not expected or supposed to be able to write fluid articulate features about Count Basie or Glenn Miller for the school newspaper, nor to write mystery stories for its literary magazine, nor indeed to be achieving an 82 per cent average in their course marks.

Jack did all that, and also shone as a star of Horace Mann's football team in that 1939-40 season. As the school yearbook noted admiringly: "Brain and brawn found a happy combination in Jack . . . a brilliant back in football, he also won his spurs as a *Record* reporter and a leading *Quarterly* contributor." It was a view Horace Mann's football coach, "Ump" Tewhill, readily shared, as Jack delivered a sequence of outstanding personal performances in a year that climaxed with Horace Mann beating Tome, their deadliest rivals, for the first time in many years.

And guess who scored the only, and winning, touchdown to become the hero of the hour?

Returning to Lowell for the summer after graduation from Horace Mann—where he listened to the official ceremony from a prone position on the lawn outside the assembly hall, his funds not running to the rental of appropriate clothes—and supposedly doing repeat work on the two courses he'd failed (chemistry and, embarrassingly, the formal French that bore little relation to the patois he spoke), Jack found himself pitched instead into the brainstorming sessions of The Young Prometheans, again thanks to the insistence of Sebastian Sampas, who had grown into a frenetic livewire with a tendency to declaim Shelley, Byron or a torch-song in public places, often while standing on a café table-top.

The bonding between Jack and Sebastian was incredibly strong. They were kindred spirits in many respects, and grew so close that Gabrielle and Leo became uncomfortable and suspicious of Jack's relationship with the foppish Sebastian. It is generally agreed that their fears were groundless, however. Whatever else they shared, Jack and Sebastian were never lovers, even if Sebastian's adoration was absolute. It was founded on an admiration for Jack's burgeoning talent, as he confided to another Young Promethean, George Constantinides: he was convinced Jack was a great writer who was **"destined for great things."**

To ensure that his prediction proved correct, the precociously well-read Sebastian introduced Jack to William Saroyan and Thomas Wolfe, two writers who would both inspire and confirm Kerouac's dreams of a literary career. Thomas Wolfe especially opened Jack's eyes to the great, and mythic, open spaces of America, spaces which were waiting to be explored anew and captured afresh by someone with the eyes to see and the words to describe what he found there.

All in all, The Young Prometheans—Sebastian, Jack, Ed Tully, John "Ian" MacDonald, Jim O'Dea, Cornelius "Connie" Murphy and George Constantinides—were a remarkable group of individuals, some of whom would go on to brilliant careers, although all in very different fields. Constantinides, for instance, became a CIA field operative, and "Connie" Murphy began his career as a nuclear physicist before going on to re-train as a medical doctor, while Jim O'Dea firmly established himself as a successful lawyer in California.

September 1940 saw Jack begin his life as a Columbia University freshman, finding himself a room on campus in Livingstone Hall to end his commuting days from Brooklyn and enable him to throw himself wholeheartedly into the role of Serious College Student, adopting a sports jacket and studious pipe to add gravitas to his appearance and tuning his radio to a classical music station while he worked at his books.

He also threw himself into football training, was duly allocated the position of wingback by coach Lou Little, but languished, exasperated, on the bench for the first half of his debut game—against Rutgers University on October 12, which Columbia lost 18-7. Jack obviously did enough to please Coach Little when he eventually took the field, however, for he found himself in the starting line-up for Columbia's next game when they faced St. Benedict's Preparatory School.

Descended upon by two St. Benedict's players as he caught a punt, Jack heard a cracking sound when he tried to evade their clutches, followed by searing pain, and limped off for treatment. With his injury diagnosed as nothing worse than a sprain that would soon mend, Jack attempted to train despite increasing discomfort, the latter made worse by accusations of shamming from Lou Little. It wasn't until a belated X-ray revealed a hairline fracture of his tibia that Jack's leg was encased in plaster. His football season was over before it had really begun.

Not his first year as a Columbia student, however.

Temporarily relieved of the onerous and demeaning task of washing dishes to pay for his meals, Jack filled the time he had when not immersed in studying course books (where Greek classics played an early part in his education) by continuing the unofficial reading course that had been set by Sebastian Sampas.

above the lovely LuAnne Henderson—Jack Kerouac's future lover and child bride of Neal Cassady.

The core authors, William Saroyan and Thomas Wolfe, provided Jack with very different, but equally valuable, lessons. Like Jack, Saroyan had been raised speaking a language other than English (in his case Armenian) and had largely taught himself to master his country's mother tongue. His mastery of that, and the consummate skill he displayed in his short stories, proved inspirational. Similarly, the more Jack was to investige Wolfe's evocative descriptions of the wild American landscape, the more he was convinced that his future lay in attempting his own pen portraits of the world out there awaiting discovery.

Then there was Jack London, another self-educated novelist who had dedicated most of his writing career to describing the grandeur of frontier America and had made much of his way around and across the country by the simple and romantic expediency of hopping freight trains.

Jack learned that London had expanded his vocabulary by actively seeking new words, writing them on pieces of paper and sticking them to mirrors as memory aids. It was an invaluable tip for a young man desperate to increase his own command of English and Jack's Livingtone Hall room soon became appropriately bedecked with similar notes to himself as he composed essays or wrote a mass of letters home to family and friends.

Exclusion from football training also gave Jack time to continue his investigation of New York—the jazz clubs, art museums and galleries, art movies and stage dramas . . . and the seamy, exciting night-life of Times Square, 42nd Street and the Harlem bars and clubs where hookers, pimps and other hustlers lived their lives under flickering neon lights.

His sexual explorations were actively pursued here, too, with black prostitutes proving an especial attraction and one he was ready to share with his Lowell buddies when they came to call. In September 1940, for example, Jack, Scotty Beaulieu and GJ Apostolos all had sex with a girl called Lucille at the New American Hotel. Seven months later he would write telling Sebastian, who was now at Boston's Emerson College, that he and GJ had "possessed the bodies of a few women" when Apostolos weekended with him.

During the summer of 1941 Jack dated Mary Carney again and explored Boston with Sebastian, the two of them hitch-hiking and Jack learning the thrills of serendipity. Would their ride be in a truck, a beat-up family saloon or a farmer's flatbed; the driver voluble, monosyllabic, bright or stupid? Whatever, they all had stories to tell, or philosophies you could listen to, learn from or deride with giggles, later. It may be no more than a 25-mile trip, but that road to Boston offered so many possibilities. Imagine, then, what mysteries and adventures lay on the highways that stretched to California, Florida or Texas.

Before returning to Columbia, Jack helped his mother pack their household possessions for a move to West Haven, Connecticut. Leo had found a job as a printer there, renting an apartment that Jack described in a letter to Nin as "a hole . . . worse than anything on Moody Street or Little Canada. The sight of it made Ma sick." Storing their furniture, they rented a cottage in the Seabluff area for $40 a month. Although three-and-a-half miles out of town, it was handily near a trolley-car stop. Best of all, Jack told Nin: "Every time you look out the parlor window you can see the ocean, and sometimes the high tide splash sprays over the sea wall across the street . . ."

In September, back at Columbia and fully expecting to stroll onto any

team coach Lou Little put together, Jack was furious to learn that he was not going to start the first game of the season. After a stand-up row with Little, Jack stormed out, packed a suitcase, took the subway to his Uncle Nick's house in Brooklyn and headed for the Greyhound bus station on Eighth Avenue where he bought a ticket for Washington DC.

Jack Kerouac had quit Columbia University and was on the road for the first time.

2 1941-1946

THE SEA, THE TOWN AND THE CITY

Even though Jack would later describe his decision to leave Columbia as the most important of his life, the letter he wrote Sebastian from the cheap hotel room he'd rented in Washington reflected his true feelings at the time, during what would only be a day-long trip. He was, he admitted, "afraid to go home, too proud and too sick to go back to the football team." Worse, he was "lonely, sick, and cried."

Swallowing hard—and fearful of the outraged response his news would bring—Jack headed for West Haven to tell his parents that his academic and football careers were over and that he intended to become a writer. Leo's wrath was fuelled by his inability to understand how his son could be so stupid, unthinking and reckless.

For once, Leo Kerouac was absolutely correct. Jack's hurt at being left out of the Columbia football team was a matter he ought to have settled in an adult fashion with coach Lou Little, rather than react like a petulant, spoiled child. Jack knew in his heart that his father was right—he'd allowed his row with Little to blow out of all proportion and had leaped before he thought clearly, let alone looked. It would not be the last time Jack's often inflated sense of pride would push him into actions he almost instantly regretted but was unable to rectify with apologies.

Incapable of coping with the acrimonious atmosphere in West Haven, Jack left to stay with a friend in Hartford, Connecticut, taking on a job in a gas station. This afforded him plenty of time to read and begin writing a batch of short stories – efforts which, he was the first to admit, owed a heavy literary debt to Ernest Hemingway and William Saroyan.

Shortly after Thanksgiving, Jack's parents moved back to Lowell and a house on Gershom Avenue, in Pawtucketville. Hostilities with his father had eased during his absence, so Jack now felt able to return to his spiritual home and a job as a sports reporter on *The Lowell Sun*.

Far greater hostilities—thanks to the Japanese attack on Pearl Harbor on December 7, 1941—led Jack to announce, to everyone's surprise, that he intended to serve his country in the navy. Fired from the *Sun* when he failed to carry out a pre-arranged interview, and awaiting his enlistment papers, Jack once more headed for Washington D.C., where G.J. Apostolos was working on the vast construction site at Arlington, Virginia, which would become the Pentagon military command complex.

Jack took a job on the site but was soon fired for constant absences (the Virginia countryside proving a more attractive subject for his attention) and became a short-order cook at a diner, before making plans to hitchhike south to Thomas Wolfe's birthplace, in Asheville, North Carolina.

He also enjoyed a brief but passionate liaison with a waitress, who regaled him with tales of her hometown of Macon, Georgia, and let him play with her deck of pornographic playing cards. She was, according to G.J., only one of a number of women with whom Jack slept at that time, his sexual appetite having become almost gluttonous. Returning to Lowell, Jack wrote an apologetic letter to Lou Little, asking if Little would have him back. Although reconciliation appeared possible, failure in a first-year chemistry course meant that Jack's scholarship had been withdrawn. He would need to find $400 while his reinstatement was negotiated—an sum of money he had no chance of raising.

A chance meeting with a merchant seaman informed Jack that shipping companies were paying as much as $2,000 to those making a five-month round-trip delivering much-needed supplies to Russia. Sensing an answer to his problem, Jack headed for Boston, where he applied for a passport and became a member of the National Maritime Union. Every day he joined other hopefuls at the Union Hall looking for employment. It was not until early July that he was taken on, and on July 18 he began life as a kitchen scullion—the lowest form of marine life—on board the *S.S. Dorchester* as she sailed for Greenland with a cargo of dynamite, industrial equipment and hundreds of construction workers.

Jack's personal cargo included reading material (H.G. Wells, copies of *The Shadow*, Thomas Mann and some classics) and a stash of notebooks in which he planned to jot down his impressions of life on the high seas. These notes, he believed, would form the skeleton of his first novel and enable him—as he told Norma Blickfelt, a one-time girlfriend—to return to Columbia **"with a feeling that I am a brother of the earth, to know that I am not snug and smug in my little universe."**

There was nothing snug about that trip. Twice the *Dorchester* came under threat of German U-boat torpedo attack, a fate her sister ship, the *S.S. Chatham*, did not escape, being sunk in the Belle Isle Strait between Newfoundland and Labrador just as she entered the Atlantic on the outward leg of the voyage. Indeed, the *Dorchester* herself would join the casualty lists on her next trip when she went down in Baffin Bay with the loss of more than 1,000 lives, some of them Jack's new-made buddies. Memories of the muffled sound of depth charge explosions would resurface in *Vanity of Duluoz* 26 years later, his description of the experience characteristically vivid, as if they had been heard only hours before.

If Jack's sexual adventures had been exclusively heterosexual until now, it was on the *Dorchester* that he had his first homosexual encounter. Or, as he graphically put it during a conversation in the late Sixties with Lowell friend and biographer, Charles Jarvis, who was born and baptized Konstantinos Efthimios Ziavras: **"I got buggered once when I was a handsome lad sailing as a scullion on the high seas . . . I was corn-holed by a nasty, lecherous fatso cook who deflowered me."**

There is also some evidence to suggest that Kerouac's initiation to gay sex came when he hitched a ride from Lowell to Boston in the same year and the driver asked if he could give Jack a blow-job. Intrigued and interested, Jack agreed, later confessing to an astonished Columbia friend that "it felt good," even when a man performed the act.

There is little doubt that Jack's youthful curiosity played as great a role in these episodes as any prevailing homosexual tendencies, and he seemed to be successfully subscribing to the adage that "you should try everything at least once, except folk-dance and incest."

But there was certainly nothing but heterosexual mayhem in the few riotous days Jack and Sebastian Sampas spent in New York when the *Dorchester* docked in October. Besides witnessing the heights to which Charlie Parker and Dizzy Gillespie were now taking their music, Jack was able to introduce his drama student soulmate to the joys of the city's more dubious attractions—the whores of Harlem especially, along with the many bartenders and club owners who were just as keen to relieve Jack of his sailor's pay. While he had a good time, Sebastian was concerned by the amount of drink and drugs Jack was consuming while they tore up the town.

It was a concern others would express in the next few months when Jack returned to Columbia, the rift with Lou Little healed and his place in the college's football squad assured. Unfortunately, that would not prove true of his place in the starting line-up. When Little left him out of the team to face the Army in December—which included Henry Mazur, one of Jack's greatest rivals in Lowell High days and a man he was keen to face in combat one more time—Jack decided to put his education on hold and spend the rest of the war as a sea-dog.

Before he left Columbia again, Jack was to have two important encounters. The first, a reunion with Henri Cru, his old Horace Mann school friend, saw the re-cementing of a friendship that had begun with the hilarity of them trying to communicate in French, a language they both notionally spoke fluently but which failed to connect in the gulf that lay between Jack's "joual" and the words that came from Cru's Paris-educated mouth. The second—Henri's introduction to Jack of Edith "Edie" Parker— was to lead to Jack's first marriage.

Like Jack, Cru had recently returned from a spell of duty at sea. In July 1942 Cru had shipped out from Norfolk, Virginia, on a freighter bound for New Zealand and Australia. He had been laid off when the ship finally docked in Los Angeles and returned to New York, like Jack, in October. It was there that Cru met and began an affair with Edie Parker.

Every account of Edie Parker portrays her as a vivacious, attractive (**". . . a body as hard as an Olympic gymnast . . . and the sexiest pair of legs I've seen,"** according to Henri Cru) and adventurous young woman. Although not promiscuous, the Michigan-born heiress dispensed her favors fairly freely. She had arrived in New York late in 1941, persuading her divorced mother that this was the place to finish her high school education and embark on the artistic career she planned.

Living with her grandparents in the Fairmount apartments complex on West 11th Street, Edie disliked the high school she was attending and began, instead, to spend her hours in the West End Bar, across the street from the main Columbia University campus on Broadway. The hang-out of choice for many of Columbia's more adventurous students, the West End would eventually become the haunt of many of the writers and artists who would form the nucleus of the so-called Beat Generation—Kerouac, Allen Ginsberg and Lucien Carr included. While Henri Cru and Edie Parker could never agree where they actually met (he always said it was the West End, while she preferred an elevator in the Fairmount, where Cru's mother also had a flat), they nevertheless soon became lovers. That was certainly the state of play when Cru and Jack Kerouac were reunited.

left home is the sailor . . . a merchant mariner heads for the New York Seamen's Church Institute.

below Jack preferred Harlem, its bars, booze, music and girls—all ready to relieve a sailor of his pay.

EDIE PARKER

Having decided to spend his war service in the Merchant Marine, Cru found himself obliged to accept the next trip he was offered early in January 1943 and asked Jack to chaperone Edie while he was away. The three met in Jack's Columbia dorm before lunching at the New York Delicatessen, where Edie reputedly devoured six sauerkraut hot dogs—a feat she claimed helped capture Jack's heart!

Certainly, it was enough to inspire an ardent love letter from him the next day and, when Henri Cru sailed off, for Edie and Jack to finally become lovers. The constant nymph that she was, Edie continued to write loving letters to Henri for some time to come, he remaining blissfully unaware of the deceit being perpetrated.

When Jack quit Columbia for the last time and returned to Lowell, Edie discovered that she was pregnant. Uncertain whether Henri or Jack was the father, she told her grandmother and submitted to an abortion.

Unaware of this impending drama, Jack had spent an enjoyable Christmas with Seymour Wyse in Lowell. They took in some baseball games and met up with Sebastian—"a nice man," recalled Wyse. Now studying accountancy at New York University, Wyse helped Jack to devise a card game, which they intended to patent but was destined only to provide Jack with hours of pleasure. Readers of *Desolation Angels*—Jack's later account of the solitary weeks he spent as a fire warden in the Cascade Mountains—have the onerous task of absorbing a mass of tiresome detail concerning the said game's somewhat labyrinthine rules.

Seymour also had ample time to observe the Kerouac household. He did not take to Leo greatly and thought Gabrielle "a very dominating woman" who did not seem to communicate with anyone except her son whom, he noted, seemed "very much under her influence."

Wyse left for the Canadian Air Force, though he would spend his furloughs in Manhattan, where high jinks and jazz club outings continued

—he would give Jack an invaluable introduction, six years later, to Jerry Newman, a jazz label owner and record producer. Jack took a job parking cars at Lowell's Hotel Garage and began working in earnest on his first full-length novel, which he entitled The Sea Is My Brother. Painstakingly written in his best script, it was never to see the light of day.

As Jack was to concede, his sub-Jack London, sub-Joseph Conrad saga of the Martin brothers—Big Slim, Peter and Wesley—simply didn't make it; it was "a crock" as literature, even if it could be considered a "beautiful work" as a hand-printing exercise. Allen Ginsberg, who had sight of it a few years later, concurred: ". . . it was like heavy Germanic symbolic prose . . . there wasn't much naturalistic plot."

Boot camp March 1943—Jack's 21st birthday—brought the long-expected invitation from Frank Knox, U.S. Navy Secretary, to report for training at boot camp in Newport, Rhode Island. Jack had tried to enlist as

above left the vivacious Edie Parker (". . . a body as hard as an Olympic gymnast," according to her lover, Henri Cru). Edie was destined to become Jack's first wife in an ill-fated marriage.

left the real women in Jack's life—his sister Caroline ("Nin") and mother, Gabrielle, at home in the late 1940s.

a pilot in the Naval Air Force but failed the medical. He also failed to accept the many petty disciplines he encountered in Newport. Jack was, in his own mind at least, a seasoned mariner, so brain-numbing periods of small-arms drill and the insufferable, inescapable company of callow kids were bound to burn out his notoriously short fuse.

And so it proved one day when, during an interminable period of drill, Jack simply laid his rifle down and walked off to the camp library. He was quietly reading there when he was arrested and questioned, his answers persuading the officer concerned to have him consigned to the care of a naval psychiatrist, who diagnosed his young patient's condition as "dementia praecox"—what is now termed schizophrenia—when Jack protested his literary ambitions and admitted that, all in all, he felt more comfortable in the company of men than women.

This snap diagnosis matched Jack's own feelings about the internal conflict that saw the all-action, sporty side of his character constantly competing with the sensitive, creative soul who wanted nothing more than the inspiration of art, literature and music. As he confided to G.J. Apostolos in a letter, **". . . all my youth I stood holding two ends of rope, trying to bring both ends together in order to tie them. Sebastian was at one end, you on the other, and beyond both of you lay the divergent world of my dual mind . . ."**

When his father visited Jack, he told his son that he was right to avoid joining a war that had been caused by the great global conspiracy of communist Jewry. As ever, Leo was miles wide of the mark: Jack wanted to "do his bit" as a proudly patriotic American. It was the bullshit of service life that he loathed.

Jack ensured that his service life was at an end by running naked through an inspection parade being staged for visiting brass. Discharged from the navy in May for being a man of "indifferent character," Jack made for New York and, five months later, joined the crew of the S.S. *George Weems*, a freighter bound for Liverpool with a load of bombs. During that summer he resumed his relationship with Edie, who was now living with a friend, Joan Vollmer Adams, on West 119th Street. A journalism student, Joan was a temporary bachelor-girl, her husband Paul being away on military duty.

Edie had not exactly lived a nun-like existence since Jack's departure the previous December, but she had at least appraised Henri Cru of her dalliance with Kerouac, which created an acrimonious rift that would never heal. When she confessed to her abortion, Jack was reportedly furious but eventually forgiving, especially as the question of paternity remained unanswered. While she and Jack were now free to be open about their affair, they seem to have agreed for it to be an open-ended relationship, for both occasionally dated others.

Truth be told, Jack was in no position to begin a live-in affair with Edie, even if he had wanted one. His father having found a printing job in New York, Jack's parents relocated to Ozone Park, Queens, near Idlewild Airport (now John F. Kennedy Airport), where Gabrielle also found employment in a factory making military footwear. They appear to have been happier here than they had for years and Jack was not going to rock the boat by refusing their offer of room and board, especially as they had gone to the trouble of bringing his writing desk all the way from Lowell. Jack now divided his time between the vastly differing worlds of Manhattan and Ozone Park.

A few weeks before he shipped out for England, Jack helped Edie and Joan Vollmer Adams move home, into apartment 62 at 421 West 118th Street, when Joan's existing lease expired. Jack's commitment to Edie was reinforced by his being a co-signatory to the new lease and this apartment was destined to become a home away from home for innumerable players in the artistic revolution that coalesced into the Beat Movement.

As before, Jack carried a load of reading matter with him when he embarked on the *George Weems*.

As befitted a man about to visit Britain for the first time, he concentrated on English novelists—Hugh Walpole and Radclyffe Hall included. But it was John Galsworthy's three-novel series, The Forsyte Saga, which captured his imagination most and would inspire in him the ambition to create his own group of novels that would interconnect to form what he called "one grand tale." This, in effect, was the true genesis of what would become The Legend of Duluoz.

During his brief stop-over in England, Jack took a train from Liverpool to London, caught a classical concert at the Royal Albert Hall and reportedly spent the rest of the night with a fur-coated hooker who stole all his money. Meanwhile, back in New York, Edie and Joan were completing the task of calling on Gabrielle and Leo in Ozone Park to collect Jack's treasured collection of jazz records. Gabrielle would never take to the self-confident young woman she first met on this occasion, believing that she was too independent for her own (and her beloved Jacky's) good. Too much of a party animal and too few inclinations to be a dutiful home-maker, in fact.

Jack returned to New York early in October and headed straight for West 118th Street. Reunion with Edie was followed by discussions of marriage and a week-long trip to Michigan for Jack's formal introduction to Edie's parents in Grosse Point. They seem to have accepted their daughter's choice of partner only cautiously. Jack's parents, especially Gabrielle, were also reluctant to accept Edie. Worse, Edie was seriously underwhelmed by her first sight of Lowell when Jack took her there, triumphantly exhibiting his beautiful "trophy" to all and sundry.

The greatest hurdle of all, however, lay in Jack's insistence that they should live with his parents when they were married. As Edie had avoided spending Christmas Day with the Kerouacs, and Gabrielle's manner towards Edie never thawed beyond frosty politeness, this was a strange demand, which left Edie "horribly upset," as she told her mother.

For his part, Jack was also upset and initially jealous of a young Columbia art student Edie had met and befriended while he was away. Like Edie, Lucien Carr was attending the drawing classes of George Grosz, the eminent artist now in wartime exile from Nazi Germany. Lucien also came from a

ALLEN GINSBERG

above the young Allen Ginsberg: "The wimpiest-looking wimp," says Carolyn Cassady.

right Jack with Lucien Carr at Columbia University, 1944, before murder and mayhem.

wealthy family—in his case an engineering dynasty in St. Louis, Missouri, with links to the Rockefellers via an aunt's marriage. Worse, when Jack finally met this exciting, witty, well-travelled and precociously sophisticated newcomer, he discovered him to be angelically handsome with startling green eyes and fair hair worn boyishly long to add a touch of vulnerability he rightly suspected most women—and some men—found adorable.

Despite twinges of natural jealousy, Jack also fell under Lucien Carr's spell, especially when the 19-year-old revealed an abiding love for and comprehensive knowledge of the works of two French literary masters close to Jack's heart, the novelist Gustave Flaubert and Symbolist poet Arthur Rimbaud. Better still, Lucien was a practical joker and prodigious drinker who had perfected the art of having a good time. Even more important, he was clearly in love with Cline Young, a Barnard College student he would often bring along on double dates with Jack and Edie.

Another person Lucien would introduce to Jack and Edie, and one who would play a crucial role in Jack's life, came under Lucien's spell during the Christmas holidays of 1943. Electing to stay in New York for Christmas and New Year, Lucien was ensconced in his room at the Union Theological Seminary (Columbia's halls of residence having been commandeered by naval officer-students) listening to some music when his reverie was disturbed by a knock on the door and the sight of a slender, large-eared and bespectacled Jewish boy who wanted to know what the music was. His name, he said, was Allen Ginsberg.

A closet homosexual—and still a virgin—the 17-year-old Ginsberg was smitten by what he later described as "the most angelic-looking kid." He was thrilled when that first encounter became a firm friendship which led, only a month later, to an introduction to Jack Kerouac, when another spark was ignited by recognition of a shared tendency to cut away from mundane realities and observe "living people" like a silent ghost.

Ginsberg knew about ghosts—his mother, Naomi, was schizophrenic and communed nervously with the voices that filled her head. When she died, in 1956, he began work on *Kaddish*, an epic poem of grief-filled remembrance, which would not be completed and published until five years later. His father, Louis, was a lyrical poet, teacher and fervent socialist who encouraged his young son's early ambitions to become a lawyer specialising in employment law—a path Allen's older brother, Eugene, was already following at Columbia.

By the time he enrolled there, however, Ginsberg had begun to "out" his artistic dreams, which were being encouraged and awakened by the English courses of two professors, Mark van Doren and Lionel Trilling. In time, Jack would characterize Ginsberg as "the sweetest man in the world."

Less welcome as a new Carr-related acquaintance was David Kammerer, a 33-year-old homosexual who had been fixated on Lucien since the latter, at the age of 10, had joined the St. Louis scout group run by Kammerer. Their fathers had been business partners until Lucien's father died. At that time Kammerer was a physical education instructor and the family connection led Lucien's mother to give Kammerer permission to take her son on a holiday to Mexico, when Lucien was only 14. It was there that Kammerer made his first physical advances and a confused Lucien discovered that alcohol helped to

LUCIEN CARR

dispel the confusion he felt. Lucien appears to have accepted Kammerer's continued presence in his life patiently, feeling sorry for the man while treating him like a personal jester. Certainly, there is no evidence that he ever reciprocated Kammerer's feelings.

When Lucien moved school to Massachusetts Kammerer followed him, and thereafter to Brunswick, Maine and the University of Chicago, taking a variety of menial jobs to pay his way. In fact, he was employed as a janitor in Greenwich Village when Jack first met him at the West End Bar, sitting with Lucien in a booth. Kammerer worked his way into Lucien's ever-expanding circle of friends and served them best by introducing them to another, much older St. Louis associate, the redoubtable William Burroughs.

Named after his grandfather, who had invented the first commercial adding machine and was founder of the giant Burroughs Corporation, William Burroughs came from a family that—while it did not benefit directly from that corporate milch cow—was wealthy enough to qualify as very rich indeed.

Educated at Harvard, where he had studied anthropology and literature, Bill Burroughs went on to study psychology at Columbia University and medicine in Vienna before exploring the twilight world of the homosexual low-life to be found in the less salubrious parts of the cities he lived in. He had also spent some time in various psychiatric hospitals, as an in-patient, when he cut off the end joint of his little finger to prove his love for a man who had thrown him over.

Jack Kerouac was fascinated by Burroughs' take on life, even though he later told Nin: **"Nobody can actually like Burroughs. . . he's a cold fish all right."** Only by involving oneself in the lowest forms of humanity, the older man reasoned, could one truly say that one had lived and express opinions about such things. It did not take long for both men to agree that—as Bob Dylan would write, almost 20 years later—to live outside the law you must be honest. Or, at least, be more pure than those who conformed to the strictures and mores of an unarguably corrupt society. In such thinking lay the foundations of what would emerge as Beat philosophy.

Shortly after his birthday, Jack received devastating news: Sebastian Sampas had died of wounds received during the Allied landing at Anzio, a German stronghold north of the Italian city of Naples. Hospitalized in Algiers, North Africa, like thousands of others who had been pinned down by ferociously superior fire-power, Sebastian finally succumbed to his injuries, never to realise the full potential of his superior intelligence and wit.

Jack wrote a strange, sad letter of farewell to his dead friend, half in English, half in "joual": **"Jadis! Jadis! Jadis, on etait ensemble, non? Ensemble! Ce grand môt d'amour. . . "** (**"A long time, a very long time ago, we were together, right? Together! This great name for love. . ."**) and ending, **"Sebastian, really, your death has never ceased making of me a damned sentimentalist like yourself. . . You bastard, you, I shan't ever forgive you. Fraternally, Jean."**

The Sampas connection was not destined to end there, of course. Through the years Jack continued to see and communicate with Stella, Sebastian's younger sister, and she in turn would provide the support Jack

above jokers wild: Hal Chase, Jack, Allen Ginsberg and William Burroughs play up for the camera at Morningside Heights in 1944.

left Jack and Nin at home in Lowell, in 1940/41. He was never keen to pose for photographs, and here Jack's body language says it all.

needed when she became his third wife during his last tragic years when his mother had become incapacitated by a stroke.

In some ways, Bill Burroughs became the new Sebastian for Jack, lending him and Allen Ginsberg recommended reading from his crammed-to-overflowing bookshelves—

Kafka, Apollinaire, Nietzsche, Cocteau . . . and William Blake, the mystic English poet and artist whom Burroughs adored and whose influence would impact greatly on Ginsberg's future work and thinking. They soaked it all up greedily, with Jack thrilling to the realisation that he was no longer alone. There were kindred spirits with whom he could both communicate and, maybe, help challenge and influence American society for the better.

In May 1944 Jack headed to New Orleans in a fruitless attempt to find a ship bound for South American ports or the Caribbean, and returned to New York dejected. He desperately needed to find paid employment and in June was delighted when efforts he had made to work as a film script synopsis writer bore fruit in the form of a job offer from Columbia Pictures. Wearing obligatory suit and tie, Jack took his place among the star-struck occupants of Columbia's offices in the Rockefeller Center, with his own secretary and office. Things were looking up at last, though they were soon at rock bottom again.

The night of August 13 brought high drama and scandal when David Kammerer sought out Lucien Carr at the West End Bar and suggested a walk in Riverside Park. Lucien agreed, even though Kammerer had only recently made violent threats to Cline Young, telling her he would kill himself if Lucien did not return his love. While they talked on a park bench, Kammerer's nine years of pent-up emotions overflowed and he tried to rape Lucien. In the ensuing tussle, Lucien produced a pocketknife and stabbed his attacker twice in the heart.

Lucien then did something very stupid. In an understandable state of panic, he dragged Kammerer's corpse to the river's edge, tied his hands and feet together with shoelaces, attached rocks to the still-bleeding body with strips of the dead man's shirt and pitched him into the Hudson. It was only after this that he thought to contact Bill Burroughs, tell him what had happened and ask his advice. Burroughs suggested he should find a lawyer and inform the police.

Instead, Lucien headed for Jack's apartment and the two went for a drink, threw Lucien's knife into a drain, buried Kammerer's spectacles in Morningside Park, took in a movie and then strolled around the Museum of Modern Art. Only then did Lucien confess all to his aunt, who immediately called the family's lawyers. One of their partners accompanied Lucien when he turned himself in. It wasn't until a day later that David Kammerer's body was dragged from the Hudson River and Lucien's garbled confession was finally believed, even though he had led the homicide officers to the drain where he had dumped the murder weapon (which was never found) and the spot where his victim's glasses lay in their shallow grave.

Lucien was formally charged with the murder at the Elizabeth Street police station, and Jack Kerouac was held as a material witness, his bail

left bisexual hustler and petty thief Herbert Huncke—"Man, I'm beat!"

center Jazz giant Charlie Parker—his revolutionary phrasing inspired Jack's "bop prosody."

right Joan Vollmer Adams, whose apartment was the New York "home" of the Beat Generation.

eventually being set at $2,500—half what the judge originally levied, and the same amount that Burroughs' father had paid when he flew in from St. Louis to bail Bill out and take him back to Missouri. Jack's father Leo was incandescent with rage ("No Kerouac has ever been involved in a murder!") and simply refused to help.

Edie's family came to the rescue, but only on condition that she and Jack formalize their relationship with marriage. Reluctantly—for both would have preferred to continue the very un-formal way they lived—arrangements were hurriedly made and on August 22 Jack was taken from his Bronx County Jail cell to the local Municipal Building where Cline Young acted as Edie's bridesmaid and Jack's armed guards served as witnesses. A round of drinks was permitted in a bar, after which Jack was whisked back to jail to spend his wedding night wondering what the hell he had done.

It was not until August 30 that Jack's bail was reduced and paid. A few days later, he and Edie travelled to Grosse Point in a train so full that they were forced to ride in the baggage car. According to Edie, Jack used the flag-covered casket of a soldier as a seat. Life in Michigan was stultifying for both of them after the fun and games of Manhattan bohemia and Jack soon responded to the come-hither glances of Jane Beebe, one of Edie's friends. Edie, deeply hurt, replied with two affairs of her own. It was obvious that their marriage was over before it had a chance to begin.

While in Grosse Point Jack worked as a ball-bearing inspector in Detroit, a job his new mother-in-law arranged with a neighbor, Dick Freuhauf, who owned a trailer factory. Jack hated it, of course, but it did help him begin repaying the Parkers' $2,500 and return to New York a free man. Joan Vollmer Adams had a new five-bedroomed apartment at 419 West 115th Street and he readily accepted her offer of a place to lay his head. One by one, the usual suspects re-gathered under this new roof. Including Edie, in time, but excluding Lucien Carr.

On September 15 Lucien pleaded guilty to the manslaughter of David Kammerer and, on October 6, was sentenced to an indeterminate term in

BILL BURROUGHS

above Jack in mortal danger from Bill Burroughs' deadly Moroccan dagger! Perhaps Burroughs had learned that Jack once described him as "a cold fish alright—no one could actually like Bill."

right Another uneasy pose for the camera, in 1944.

Elmira Reformatory. The length of his sentence, he was advised, depended entirely on his response to the psychiatric counselling that he would receive. If he did not show any signs of rehabilitation, he could languish for up to 15 years in prison. Lucien was smart enough to comply and would be released only two years later.

Jack decided to return to sea, signed up on the *S.S. Robert Treat Paine* but jumped ship in Norfolk, Virginia, when the bosun began making romantic overtures. Allen Ginsberg claimed that Jack gave him his first homosexual experience about this time by masturbating him under the support columns of the West Side Highway. Any hopes Ginsberg had nurtured of a long-term romantic relationship with Jack were shattered when Jack asked him to help in the attempted seduction of Cline Young. This was something Jack claimed to have achieved when he wrote *Visions of Cody* six years later but, confusingly, said he didn't in *Vanity of Duluoz*, realising at the last moment that to do so would be to betray Lucien.

Returning to West 115th Street, Jack joined Joan's ever-expanding menagerie, which now featured Hal Chase, an anthropology student from Denver, and, occasionally, Vickie Russell, an attractive redheaded hooker who introduced the gang to the dubious pleasures of benzedrine, the amphetamine-based chemical in which the blotter strips of nasal inhalers were soaked in those days. Taken out of the inhalers, rolled into balls and swallowed with a coffee chaser, they produced a high that could last for hours. The come-down was horrible, though, and only cured by the repeated ingestion of more "bennies," or "speedballs." Jack was soon using benzedrine on a regular basis and storing up trouble for himself.

Another regular visitor to Joan's apartment was Herbert Huncke, a bisexual drug addict and thief Bill Burroughs had met during one of his late-night trawls of Times Square after he found himself in possession of a submachine gun and a stack of morphine ampoules. Vickie Russell's boyfriend, Bob Brandenberg, suggested he try to off-load them on Huncke, and Burroughs found himself immersed in the subterranean world in which Huncke, his friend Phil White and the pimps, hookers, junkies and assorted losers and hustlers carved out a nefarious living. It was Huncke who gave Bill Burroughs the first morphine shot that helped pitch him into full-blown heroin addiction. Ginsberg, too, would dabble with morphine but managed to avoid getting hooked.

Huncke, whom Jack described as having **"the look of a man who is sincerely miserable in the world,"** always claimed that it was he who introduced the word "beat" into Jack's vocabulary. While Huncke used it to express extreme weariness ("Man, I'm beat!"), Jack chose to play mind-games with the word, deciding that it could be used to encapsulate all those people living on society's edge, the beatific poor and dispossessed who nevertheless were, as he put it, **"being illuminated and having illuminated ideas about apocalypse and all that."**

This romantic notion—and an all-abiding sympathy for those who had either been failed by the system or had deliberately elected to live outside it—is a core element of Beat literature and philosophy, its principal creators believing that a new, purer way of life and spirituality could be achieved only if the old ways were rejected. It was an idealism that was, alas, destined to find few adherents among those of their own generation (including a scornfully dismissive Burroughs) but that would provide inspiration—albeit often misplaced—for the next, and give rise to the late 1960s "love and peace" ethos of the hippies.

Jack and Burroughs did find common cause, for a while at least, in the creation of a novel inspired by the Lucien Carr case. Begun in December 1944, *And the Hippos Were Boiled in Their Tanks* (a title inspired by an ". . . and finally" radio news item about a circus fire that Burroughs had heard) would become a three-month collaboration in which each partner wrote alternate chapters, both using a Dashiell Hammett tough-guy "voice." It would go no further than the desk of an editor at Simon and Schuster, however, and so did not make them the fortune they naively believed it would. What it did do, however, was convince Burroughs that the art of writing was no great mystery.

Meanwhile, Jack's own writing had taken on fresh life. Having laid *The Sea is My Brother* aside, and before he and Burroughs worked on their joint doomed enterprise, Jack began a punishing benzedrine-fuelled schedule only interrupted for twice-weekly meetings with Ginsberg to exchange library books and have a drink at the West End Bar. Most, if not all his work from that period was destroyed at the end of every day, Jack refusing to allow anything to survive that did not achieve the purity of art he was now attempting to attain.

March 1945 brought excitement in the form of Ginsberg's suspension from Columbia. On the evening of March 16, Jack had called on Allen in his Livingstone Hall room. As their talk lengthened into the small hours, William Lancaster—Allen's room-mate—hit the sack in his own room, leaving the interconnecting door ajar. Jack and Allen eventually followed suit, sleeping chastely apart with Allen in pyjamas and Jack in his underwear. They were awoken at 8am by an irate assistant dean who was following up a complaint from Ginsberg and Lancaster's cleaning lady, whom Allen suspected of anti-semitism but knew for certain was not very good at her job.

She had not, for instance, cleaned their windows for some time and Allen had chosen to demonstrate this fact by writing two large messages in the film of dirt: "Butler has no balls" (a jibe against Columbia's head man, Dean Butler) and "Fuck the Jews." Although Jack had managed to flee to Lancaster's now-vacant bed and hide under the covers, Dean Furman—one of Coach Lou Little's assistants—had recognized him. Hauled before the authorities, Ginsberg was charged $2.35 for Jack's unauthorized stay, informed that Jack was a lout who was "unwelcome on campus," ordered to clean the offending graffiti from his windows and told he could not return to Columbia until a psychiatric report determined that he was a person fit to grace its hallowed halls. Packing his life into a couple of suitcases, Allen joined the 115th Street circus before enlisting at the U.S. Maritime Service Center at Sheepshead Bay, Brooklyn, for three months' training.

Around that same time, in the spring, Jack made one of his many trips back to Lowell, where he was reunited with Mary Carney. Now Mrs. Ray Baxter, Mary was enduring an enforced separation from her airman husband, who had been posted to England. As he would not return home until 1946, the arrival of a baby daughter (named Judy) in September 1945 was enough

A HARVEST BOOK HB 183
$3.45 Slightly higher in Canada

BY THE AUTHOR OF
ON THE
ROAD

Jack Kerouac

The Town
AND
The City

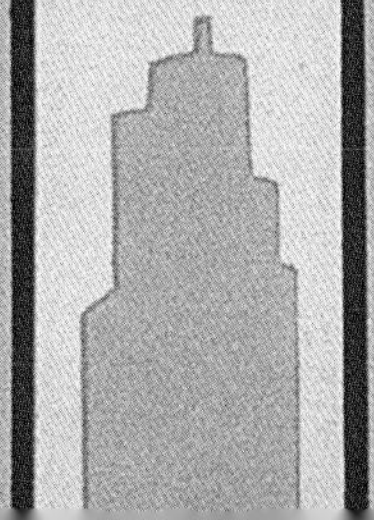

for Lowell's wagging tongues to suggest that Jack Kerouac and Mary had finally had intercourse. Mary did nothing to refute such talk, refusing to identify her daughter's sire either to her husband or the court officials who duly sanctioned Ray Baxter's divorce petition. While Judy Baxter later claimed that her mother confirmed Jack's paternity to her, Mary never made public admission of the fact.

Meanwhile, back at Joan Vollmer's apartment, Hal Chase was busying himself with a growing friendship with Jack and affairs with both Cline Young and Bill Burroughs. Destined to be characterized by Jack as a "hero of the sunny west," Chase had been recommended to Columbia by Justin Brierly, a Denver high school teacher and Columbia alumnus dedicated to spotting and encouraging promising students, and to putting them in touch with his many university connections.

But it was with Bill Burroughs that Jack spent the mid-August evening during which New York (and the rest of America) partied riotously to celebrate the Japanese surrender that marked the end of World War II. In Times Square they bumped into one of Jack's old Columbia friends, Jack Fitzgerald, and his girlfriend, Eileen. Later, while Fitzgerald slept beside them, Jack made love to Eileen for the first time to mark the beginning of an affair he conducted while attempting, once more fruitlessly, to persuade Cline Young to drop her defences. His renewed efforts were rebuffed mostly, it is fair to assume, because Cline still counted Edie as a best friend who was, after all, still married to Jack.

Ever curious about his own sexuality and still determined to investigate all experiences life had to offer, Jack continued to flirt with the gay demi-monde, accompanying Bill Burroughs or Allen Ginsberg to homosexual hang-outs and parties. He told Ginsberg that he found such activities repellent, however, and counter to everything he had been raised to believe.

Nevertheless, he conceded that **"whatever's in my subconscious is there."** After getting a summer job as a busboy at a Jewish resort hotel in the Catskills (the tips were lousy, so he quit), Jack persuaded his old boss at Columbia Pictures to re-hire him. In September Hal Chase and Bill Burroughs decided to move into Joan Vollmer's. A month later Edie, too, checked into the apartment and soon Jack returned to his wife's bed, on one of his regular returns from his parents' home in Ozone Park.

This was to be no rekindling of lost love's flame, however. Edie was appalled by the amount of drug-taking, though she tried to match Jack's increasing use of benzedrine. This caused her problems with her teeth that, combined with a diet of nothing but mayonnaise sandwiches, persuaded her to head back for the square meals and inevitable "told-you-so" nagging of her triumphant mother only a month or two later.

That autumn also saw two events that would prove momentous in Jack's life. His father was informed he had an inoperable cancer of the spleen, and Jack began work on what would eventually emerge after a three-year slog as his first published novel, *The Town and the City*. As Leo slipped into a long period of bed-ridden and pain-wracked agony, Jack upped his already prodigious ingestion of benzedrine. There was only one likely conclusion to this madness and shortly before Christmas Jack collapsed after a week-long benny-binge. He was rushed to Queens Veterans Administration Hospital with thrombophlebitis—clotting of blood in his legs, which would have proved fatal if a clot had worked its way to his heart or brain.

Ordered to rest after a two-week stay in hospital, Jack found himself spending an increasing amount of time at his dying father's bedside, the two men submerging their pain in long drinking sessions. When his father finally died during the spring of 1946, Jack was devastated. Not only by the awful reality of Leo's leaving him with the command to take care of his mother, no matter what, but with a deep remorse at having failed to live up to his father's high expectations. He had blown it as a football star. He had dropped out of university. And he was mixing with a bunch of ne'er-do-wells whom Leo and Gabrielle dismissed either as hop-heads, filthy queers or dirty Jews.

After Leo's burial in the Kerouac family plot in Nashua, (where his young son, Gerard, had also been interred), Jack spent the rest of 1946 in a flurry of guilt-driven work. Drawing on his phenomenal memory for the minutiae of his Lowell childhood, Jack returned to *The Town and the City*, giving Leo a central role as the Irish Catholic family head Robert Martin, depicting Gabrielle as the loving earth-mother Marguerite Courbet Martin, and various aspects of himself as the five Martin brothers, Joe, Francis, Peter, Charley and Mickey. The saintly Gerard became the similarly martyred Julian, while Nin's principal characteristics were given to the two Martin sisters, Ruth and Elizabeth. In truth, they bore more resemblance to the family of Sebastian Sampa, with whom Jack remained in touch.

Now living full-time with Gabrielle in Ozone Park, Jack started to work variously as a night clerk and elevator operator and, on the few occasions when he stayed at the 115th Street apartment, defied doctors' orders by supercharging his system with benzedrine, booze and marijuana.

Joan Vollmer (by now embroiled in an unlikely romantic liaison with the still mostly gay Bill Burroughs) would succumb to amphetamine psychosis and spend some time in the notorious Bellevue Hospital before being whisked off to east Texas where Burroughs planned to grow and harvest marijuana on a commercial scale. Herbert Huncke failed to dodge the law and found himself in the Bronx jail before moving out to live with Vicky Russell when he was released. With Allen Ginsberg now living for the most part with his parents in Paterson, New Jersey, a remarkable era had ended

In December 1946, however, an equally remarkable era was to begin—an era that would pitch Jack Kerouac into a thrilling, often dangerous and illuminating friendship destined to inspire him, help him find his own literary "voice" and create a modern legend.

Neal Cassady hit town.

above Jack and Hal Chase at Morningside Heights. The hat belonged to Bill Burroughs . . .

3 1947-1950

ON THE ROAD

It is pointless to ponder what might have been if Jack Kerouac had never met Neal Cassady. There can be no doubt that he would still have embarked on his odyssey to explore and derive inspiration from the vast, rich emptiness of the American heartland, just as we can be certain that he would have written about the people and places he found there. By the same token, however, his experiences—and his subsequent writings—would not have been as rich if his early questing had not been under the expert tutelage of Neal Cassady, a young man already wise to the ways of the world, and of its many long and winding roads.

Almost four years younger than Jack (he claimed to have been born in the back of a beat-up jalopy on February 8, 1926, while his parents were passing through Salt Lake City), Neal Cassady had packed enough experience into his 20 years to qualify as a seasoned, if not hardened, man. He had enjoyed no more than six years of dysfunctional family life when his parents split up and he elected to spend his summers following his alcoholic father (a barber living in a succession of bug-ridden Denver flophouses) on the fruit harvest trail, either hitching rides or hopping freight trains in search of casual work or the hospitality of friends and relatives.

Formal schooling played only a small part in Neal's life after he passed the age of 14 (though a successfully passed special test would win him a high school diploma). But the education he received in Denver pool halls supplied him with the skill to hustle a few bucks when times got especially hard. Like Jack, Neal had a prodigious memory and insatiable lust for knowledge that enabled him to soak up academic information. Thus, when he came to the attention of Justin Brierly, Neal's innate abilities and obvious intelligence marked him as worthy of Brierly's patronage and extra attention—not least because he was a terrifically good-looking young man and Brierly was an unashamedly predatory homosexual, as Hal Chase had already testified to the New York crowd.

Apparently willing to submit to Brierly's advances in return for the undoubtedly valuable education he received, Neal's schooling was inevitably disjointed as he embarked on a career as a car thief. Not for financial gain, but for the sheer pleasure of joy-riding vehicles that also served as girl-magnets, for he had discovered the joys of driving at the age of 14 and the even greater pleasures of sex some years earlier than that.

According to his own accounts (which are suspect if only because his grasp of truth was notoriously tenuous and he liked nothing better than a bit of embellishment when spinning a yarn), Neal had "borrowed" more than 500 cars between 1940 and 1944, finishing up in reform schools on a number of occasions. The last had been only a year earlier and forced him to abandon plans to join Hal Chase in New York where he hoped to use a Brierly recommendation to gain admittance to Columbia.

left Jack Kerouac's hero of the golden West.
Neal Cassady in San Francisco, 1952.

Since then, Neal had met and married the 16-year-old LuAnne
Henderson, a beautiful blonde cheerleading high-school dropout whom he
had easily swept off her feet and embroiled in his go-with-the-flow lifestyle.
They arrived in New York via Sidney, Nebraska (where LuAnne's aunt lived),
and North Platte (where the car Neal had stolen from LuAnne's employers
broke down), using some of the $300 LuAnne had stolen from her
employers to buy Greyhound bus tickets for the rest of their trip. Both
would later admit that they spent the first few hours of their stay wandering
like awestruck hayseeds among the glitter of Times Square.

They caught up with Hal Chase the following morning, with Neal
especially keen to meet the brilliant young writer Hal had told him so much
about in letters. And while that writer would describe his first meeting with
the character he renamed Dean Moriarty in *On the Road* as taking place at
Neal and LuAnne's apartment in East Harlem, they inevitably met at the
West End Bar, where Jack was only one of a crowd that included Ginsberg,
architecture student and budding novelist Alan Temko and Chase's room-
mate Ed White, both fellow Denver exiles. It was, by all accounts, not an
entirely successful encounter.

below Carolyn Cassady's 'boys': Neal and Jack get all nonchalant for posterity.

Jack and Neal had both been the recipients of much Hal Chase hype regarding the other and were cautiously suspicious. Neal also decided to play to the gallery, overdoing his West End debut with a bravura act designed to prove his reputation as an all-action wild child. But while Temko and White initially wrote him off as a loudmouth con-artist, Allen Ginsberg fell in love with the beautiful boy. Herbert Huncke also took to Neal at once, though it could be said that it takes one smooth-talking hustling charmer to recognize another, and Neal Cassady could be a complete charmer—albeit a feckless, reckless and often selfish one when the devil in him took control. That said, his devilment never seems to have been malicious.

The East Harlem meeting couldn't have been scripted more dramatically. Jack's knock on the door was answered by a stark naked Neal (given a modestly coy pair of shorts in *On the Road*) and the sight of the retreating rear of an equally nude LuAnne. Asking a suitably impressed Jack, Hal and Ed to give him a few minutes to complete his unfinished, ahem, business with his teen bride, Neal vanished behind the bedroom door, so confirming Chase's advance publicity of him as a tireless sexual athlete.

During the all-night talkathon that followed, Jack Kerouac and Neal Cassady became true soul brothers, not least because each—in many ways—possessed the very qualities the other lacked but yearned for in himself

For his part, Jack would have loved to be a madman dancing crazily to the music of the universe, only too aware that he would never be able to match Neal's boundless energy and enthusiasm, nor his apparent ability to strike up an instantaneous rapport with almost everyone he met.

And the things Jack had enjoyed—a warm, comforting childhood and a solid education—were the very same elements Neal longed for, even if he had been able to wed the opposing sides of his character by being a streetwise hustler with a back-pack full of literary classics. Jack, however, continued to struggle with a Jekyll-and-Hyde nature which had enjoyed the hero status of athletic prowess and locker room badinage while thrilling to the challenge of esoteric Young Promethean mind-games with Sebastian, Ian, Ed, Connie, Jim and George.

Bill Tomson, a boyhood friend of Neal's in Denver, has recalled the impact Jack had on Neal: "I remember getting a letter from Neal when he first went to New York, and he was calling me 'younger brother' and Jack the older brother. So Neal looked up to Jack for his tenacity and for his intellectual competence, as well as finding companionship in Jack's energy."

That companionship would be stretched in those early days as Allen Ginsberg tried to hijack all of Neal's time, partly for sexual reasons but also to help steer his studies. Determined to become a writer, Neal asked both men for advice, some of which Jack tried to give when Neal stayed briefly with him (and a reluctant, ever-supicious Gabrielle) in Ozone Park. That was after LuAnne left for Denver in March, her departure having been forced by a strange crisis of her own making.

With Neal working as a car park attendant at the New Yorker Hotel and LuAnne still suffering from the trauma of having wandered lost in Harlem through a late-night snowstorm, she told Neal that she had had a visit from the police. It was a lie, and one LuAnne has never been able to explain to anyone, least of all herself. She knew perfectly well that Neal had an understandable fear of cops, so could not have been surprised when he began packing his possessions in a frantic panic. He lived in hiding and on the run for a few days and, when he returned to their New Jersey apartment, found that LuAnne had gone.

It was only a week or later that Neal himself climbed aboard a Denver-bound bus, leaving an emotionally bereft Ginsberg and an itchy-footed Jack behind. A few days later, as Allen began to consolidate plans to move to Colorado and a hoped-for continued affair with Neal, Jack received an 800-word letter postmarked Kansas City. To his astonishment, that letter (a frank, funny and ribald account of Neal's attempted on-bus seduction of one girl and his successful conquest of another) accurately captured his friend's mile-a-minute conversational style. It broke all kinds of grammatical rules and cheerfully dispensed with correct punctuation, but it contained its author's "voice," his sense of fun and his boundless energy.

A light bulb went on in Jack's brain. Maybe this was the way to go. Forget the formal, academic, strait-laced ways of past literary masters and pitch yourself headlong into reflecting or capturing the real voices you heard, or find and use your own real voice to create work that was truly "now," and not some tired re-working of the old. It was something to think about and work at.

Jack returned to work on *The Town and the City*, fuelled with benzedrine and helped in his single-mindedness by the fact that none of his friends now remained in New York. Bill Burroughs had long since departed for Texas, Allen Ginsberg had found himself a night-cleaner's job in a Denver store in June, while Hal Chase, Alan Temko and Ed White had also returned back home to Colorado.

After a two-week holiday with his sister, Nin, and her new husband, Paul Blake, in June—which included a trip to view the primeval wonders of Georgia's Okefinokee Swamp and witnessing a fight between two black girls, one wielding a meat cleaver—Jack and Gabrielle returned to Ozone Park with Jack's plans pretty well confirmed. He was going to hitchhike to Denver to meet up with Neal, Allen and the others. Then he would head for San Francisco and a reunion with Henri Cru.

On July 17, 1947, Jack kissed "Mémère" (the family name for Gabrielle since Nin had made her a grandmother) goodbye and hit the road. Less than two days later he limped back to Manhattan, his first five rides having taken him only a few miles up the Hudson River road out of New York and a day-long rainstorm forcing him to take a bus back to the city. On to plan B, then, which involved the headstart of a first leg by bus to Chicago and a second—also by bus—to Joliet, Illinois, and his first sight of Route 6 winding its way southwest across the Midwestern plains and prairies.

Making good progress, Jack was soon sending word of the sights and sounds he was experiencing in postcards to Gabrielle (who became his "aunt"

above a San Francisco street photographer captured this shot of Carolyn Robinson and Neal Cassady in December 1947 – before they were married. Neal had just arrived from Denver.

right Carolyn Cassady's sketch of Neal at work on his memoirs in 1951.

DEAN MORIARTY

in *On the Road*) after a lifetime of having to take other people's word for it that the grainfields of Iowa and Nebraska really did stretch as far as where land meets sky in a heat-hazed blur, that the banks of the Missouri and Mississippi Rivers really were as wide as, oh, "this," and that the people he met in drugstores, bars and cheap motels—real-life cowboys in Stetsons, tractor-driving farmers, long-distance truckers, housewives, businessmen and bums—all had something to say that he could scribble into the little notebooks he habitually carried in his jacket pocket. Not that he didn't trust his fabled memory, but a contemporaneous note was certain to be spot-on as a record of that first 1,000-mile trek.

All too soon Jack had his first sight of the snowcaps incongruously fringing the Rocky Mountains, as he made his way across the last of the great plains through summer heat that made the landscape shimmer and jump . . . and there was Denver. Jack headed for Hal Chase's home for a few days before accepting Alan Temko's offer of a room in the White family house in which he and Ed were already living. To his dismay, it was a full 10 days before he was able to locate Neal and he had to find Allen Ginsberg before doing that. The Ivy League faction had not kept in touch with the merry lunatic.

Neal had entangled himself in one of his labyrinthine intrigues. Despite having been reconciled with LuAnne on his return to Denver, he was now paying court to Carolyn Robinson, a young graduate student of fine arts and theatre arts at the University of Denver whom he had met via a mutual friend, Bill Tomson, when they both visited Carolyn at her room in The Colburn, a residence hotel on Grant Street. The beautiful Carolyn epitomized the respectability Neal yearned to acquire.

Three years older than Neal, Carolyn soon became subjected to a full Cassady charm offensive, during the course of which he swore that he and LuAnne were definitely through and an annulment of their marriage was imminent. While he wore down her initial misgivings, Neal continued to see LuAnne behind her back. It would not be until she and Neal left Denver, having moved with him to a furnished room on Clarkson Street, that she learned the truth, although LuAnne was almost certainly aware of his duplicity throughout.

Neither woman, it is safe to assume, knew the sub-text of Allen Ginsberg's encouragement of Neal's dreams. Allen was, in Carolyn's words, "the wimpiest-looking wimp you had ever seen at that time." There was no chance he was also the all-male Neal's lover. To add further confusion, Neal was also secretly dallying with the affections of two waitresses, the Gyllion sisters. Jack had a one- or two-night stand with one of them, thanks to a Cassady introduction, and they would pop up pseudonomously in *On the Road* as the Bettencourts.

What with one thing and another, then, Neal didn't have too much spare time to devote to Jack during that trip, although he did take him down to the area around Larimer Street where his father had eked out his wretched alcohol-driven existence and they exchanged spooky childhood reminiscences —Jack of The Shadow-inspired Doctor Sax prowling Lowell's woods and Neal of what Ginsberg called his "bogeyman fantasies" of the horrors that maybe lurked in the dark urine-drenched alleyways of his younger years.

above Carolyn Robinson in Denver,1947. Beautiful and intelligent, she epitomised the respectability Neal Cassady yearned to acquire.

Neal did, however, serve Jack well by introducing him to two men destined to become good friends—Bill Tomson and Al Hinkle—and, naturally, introducing him to Carolyn. They liked each other immensely at first sight and the first "frisson" of what would later become a full-blown love affair took place when they danced together to a tavern jukebox Neal kept charged with quarters.

"Dancing with Jack was the only time I felt the slightest doubt about my dedication to Neal," Carolyn noted in her 1990 memoirs, *Off the Road*, **"for here was the warm physical attraction Neal lacked. This realization disturbed me and was difficult to brush away. Jack's manner was tender without being suggestive, although he did betray some tension. As though he had read my thoughts, he said softly in my ear: 'It's too bad, but that's how it is—Neal saw you first.'"**

With Henri Cru and the chance of a crewman's job beckoning, Jack telegraphed Gabrielle for a much-needed $50 and took a bus to San Francisco two weeks too late to secure the job but in time to join Henri (who was living with a girlfriend in Mill Valley) in the unlikely role of a uniformed—and armed—security guard. With the badge of a Marin County special police officer on his chest, Jack guarded the site of an international construction company's dormitory complex in Sausalito, earning the unimaginable riches of $50 a week, most of which was dutifully sent back to Ozone Park for Gabrielle's safe-keeping. Jack and Henri made their wages go further by the simple expediency of stealing food from the kitchens.

right the young graduate student faces an unimaginable future. Carolyn in 1946.

below Henri Cru in 1940. Seven years later he and Jack Kerouac would be stealing food to supplement their wages as security guards.

With unlimited access to a typewriter and company stationery, Jack thrashed out a 40,000-word screenplay Henri promised to lay on the desk of a Hollywood friend—where it duly remained—and a string of letters to Neal, Ginsberg, Lucien Carr and Burroughs, among others. There was also a disastrous dinner date with Henri's father, an eminent academic who was not impressed by the drunken slurrings of his son's friend, nor by the antics of an equally intoxicated Alan Temko, who gatecrashed the party and was ejected from the restaurant after insulting Professor Cru.

A few later, Jack began to head south, towards Los Angeles. He hitchhiked to Bakersfield, then caught a bus. It was in Bakersfield that he met Bea Franco, a strikingly beautiful migrant worker with whom he enjoyed a two-week affair, partly in a Hollywood hotel room and latterly in Selma, where Jack tried—and failed—to come up to par as a cotton picker. Although he and Bea talked of settling down together in New York, their affair ended the day they parted, Jack returning to Los Angeles where another $50 from Gabrielle enabled him to buy a bus ticket for Pittsburg. It did, however, furnish Jack with the material for a short story, entitled *The Mexican Girl*, first published in *Paris Review* and included in *On the Road*.

Resuming work on *The Town and the City*, by now a massive 280,000-word tome that would grow by another 100,000 words before he declared it finished early in 1948, Jack lived with Gabrielle in Ozone Park, their income entirely dependent on the work she found in footwear factories and the little he received from the government under the G.I. Bill. His brief spell in the U.S. Navy had not been entirely wasted, then. Importantly, Jack now began introducing the more naturalistic phrasings and structures that he and Neal had discussed in their late-night conversations and letters.

In his 1948 letters, Jack pronounced fantastical notions of using the huge publishing and movie rights advances that he imagined would come his way from *The Town and the City* to buy a ranch in California—a haven for himself, Neal, Carolyn and other like-minded souls to lead a life dedicated to growing corn and riding the range. These would, of course, come to nothing—as many other impractical Kerouac dreams were fated to fail. The best explanation for these failures is Carolyn Cassady's:

"Jack lived in a fantasy world . . . He expressed his opinions spontaneously and they often conflicted with each other. He never followed a single thread, and it's this habit of inconsistency that makes it so hard for people to determine what he actually thought." A classic Pisces . . .

The return of Bill Burroughs and Allen Ginsberg to New York saw a lift in Jack's barren social life, and together, the three careened through a whirl of parties (including guests like W.H. Auden and Ernest Hemingway, of whom Jack was too overawed to meet), jazz clubs (often with Seymour Wyse and Jerry Newman) and art gallery events (for the likes of Jackson Pollock and Larry Rivers). Along the way, the budding novelist John Clellon Holmes became part of the crowd. His interest in Jack, Allen and Bill would grow into a fascination with their work and philosophies and the use of the expression **"Beat Generation"** to categorize them and others who followed this new path.

In that fact alone there is a story, for Jack would be furious when Holmes' *Go*, unarguably the world's first glimpse of the huge artistic underground that existed by the time of its publication in 1952, stole a march on his own unpublished depictions of the same scene. Worse, Holmes used the phrase that Jack claimed to have coined first, in a moment of inspiration in 1948 when he and Holmes were discussing what their generation—and their "movement"—could be called.

Gertrude Stein had characterized the young post-World War I Parisian art and literary crowd as "The Lost Generation" and F. Scott Fitzgerald—one of those "lost" souls—had coined the later "Jazz Age" to describe the hedonistic fast times he lived in 1920s and 30s America. What phrase epitomized the new rising crowd better than "The Beat Generation," Jack ventured. Holmes could never be persuaded to recall the whoop of joy Jack always claimed John gave to greet this flash of inspiration, even if he conceded its true origin as readily as Jack did his debt to the deadbeat Herbert Huncke.

That year also saw a blooming of the "theology" of the Beats—the way they expressed the innate sanctity of the world and its dispossessed masses—and no more so than after Allen Ginsberg had what he described as a life-changing mystical experience in May. Immersed in a volume of William Blake's poetic works, in the version he told Jack (though to Carolyn he said he had been masturbating!), Ginsberg had felt as if he had heard Blake's voice uttering the verse while his apartment filled with a blinding light that revealed to him a vision **"of the entire universe as poetry . . . filled with light and intelligence and communication and signals."**

While others, including Ginsberg's father, gently suggested psychiatric help, Jack was more sympathetic. Then, as both drew on their respective religious backgrounds to articulate this new-found awareness, words such as "angels," "visions" and "holy" began to creep into their language, to be joined later by the likes of "satori," "nirvana" and "dharma" when first Ginsberg and then Jack took up their studies of Buddhism.

With *The Town and the City* finished—and almost instantly rejected by Scribner's, original publishers of Thomas Wolfe, whose influence on the book was glaringly obvious—Jack started work on two new projects: his atmospheric and haunting gothic horror-inspired novel, *Doctor Sax: The Myth of the Rainey Night*, and a long short story centered on Neal Cassady that would form the foundation of the narrative that would grow and evolve into *On the Road*.

Meanwhile, in San Francisco that April, Neal and Carolyn had become Mr. and Mrs. Cassady, their daughter Cathleen being born five months later. Neal had annulled his marriage to LuAnne (she was underage when they married) and, with Al Hinkle's help, found employment with the Southern Pacific Railroad. As he and Carolyn settled into their one-bedroomed apartment on Alpine Terrace, Neal began work on the manuscript of his own memoirs, a large chunk of which would be published posthumously in 1971 as *The First Third*. Carolyn could be forgiven for believing that Neal's wandering days were over and she had somehow tamed the tiger.

PARAMOUNT

CALIFORNIA
WESTERN
STATES
LIFE

WEINSTE

STERLING

UNITED
ARTIST

UNITED ART
GEO BERNARD SHAWS MAJOR
WENDY HILLER 2ND LA
TANKS A MILLION JAMES

She could not have been more wrong. In December, when Southern Pacific introduced seasonal lay-offs, Neal blew most of their savings on a new Hudson car and announced his intention of taking off with Al Hinkle and Helen, Hinkle's new bride, to drive across country to Rocky Mount, North Carolina, where he knew Jack and Gabrielle were going to spend the Christmas holiday with Nin and Paul Blake. Then they plannned to bring Jack back to California.

Aghast and hurt, Carolyn realized that Neal's actions were not caused by a wish to hurt her, nor by arrant selfishness. He simply had no concept of how a family man should behave, never having experienced it with his own father. In brief, says Carolyn, Neal Cassady simply **"didn't have the same frame of reference that most people had."**

However, unthinking as ever, Neal made Denver his first stop, where he made a 3 a.m. call at LuAnne's door. She, preparing for marriage to a sailor away on duty, took little persuading to join Neal on what he promised was a trip "to where we belonged." By the time they reached Tucson, Arizona, Helen Hinkle had endured enough of Neal's nerve-wracking driving and elected to travel alone to Bill Burroughs' place, leaving Al with strict orders to meet her there in two weeks. He wouldn't make it.

Neal's mud-covered Hudson pulled up at the Blake home in Rocky Mount just as Christmas dinner was being served. The car's tired and hungry occupants took little persuading to join the family feast. Learning that Mémère was set to move back to New York, Neal generously offered to help.

And so it was that he, Jack, Al and LuAnne drove to Ozone Park with a pile of Gabrielle's personal effects and, after only the briefest of turnarounds, Neal and Jack drove the 700 miles back to Rocky Mount to collect Gabrielle herself and the rest of her belongings. Just over 2,000 miles in three days through rain, wind and snow . . . the stuff of which legends are made.

The quartet spent the next three weeks in New York celebrating the arrival of 1949, much of their time carousing with Allen Ginsberg and Lucien Carr. For a while they stayed with John Clellon Holmes, whose place, according to LuAnne, became party HQ for up to a hundred people on some nights, their host trying to work through the din. It was during this idyll that Jack and LuAnne felt the first twinges of mutual attraction.

Although Neal made it obvious that he did not mind if they slept together, Jack demurred (for a while), unaware—as Carolyn Cassady explains—that "it was Neal's generous practice to share any good thing he had with those he loved, no matter who, what or which. It didn't mean that he didn't get jealous, but for that he could blame 'the gal.' "

They finally set off for California on January 19, with Jack keen to observe his new crazy-man friend in depth, and fantasising on the delights of a compliant LuAnne. True to form, Neal wore only a T-shirt as protection against the winter cold outside—or inside, for the Hudson had no heater.

Despite being less than two months old, Neal's new car was already well run-in, with twisted fenders (memento of a crash into a ditch en route from Denver) and broken windshield wipers, not to mention a dashboard which was already sagging from the constant slapping it received from Neal as he furiously beat out the tempo of tunes that continually blasted at full volume from the radio, which was always tuned to jazz or blues stations. Which was fine by Jack.

First, though, they made for Louisiana, where Bill and Joan Burroughs were now living, in Algiers, across the Mississippi River from New Orleans. They remained there only until Jack's G.I. money arrived, leaving Al Hinkle to stay on with Helen in New Orleans. When Jack's funds ran out—as Neal's had, long since—they picked up hitch-hikers and panhandled, stole food from roadside diners and gas stations and, in Arizona, pawned Jack's watch to get a dollar's worth of gasoline.

Which was also fine by Jack: nothing could spoil his thrill at being back on the American road, following the blue highways to see the real country and all who inhabited it, including the spirits of ancient native gods, white settlers and explorers.

Arriving in San Francisco, Jack was stunned when Neal pulled the car up in O'Farrell Street and told him and LuAnne to find a room together—he was off for a reunion with Carolyn and Cathleen. LuAnne took charge and persuaded the manager of the Blackstone, a cheap hotel in which she had once lived, to give them credit. After explaining to a bemused, near-tearful Jack that Neal's behavior was typical of a man who would "leave you out in the cold any time it's in his interest," she spent the next two days and nights helping him fulfill all the fantasies he had been nursing.

Both knew that the relationship was never going to develop into anything long-term, even though their lovemaking was punctuated by spells of energetic conversation. LuAnne realized that her new lover was too detached. He observed, but didn't, she thought, "get involved with the reality of it." The same was true of his relationships, in which possessiveness played no real part, and of the act of lovemaking itself, when it seemed that he appeared more interested in making mental notes of the experience than simply surrendering himself to its sensations. In that way, despite the sensuality of his physical appearance, LuAnne pronounced that Jack Kerouac "was not a sensual person."

To illustrate her argument, LuAnne recounted an episode to biographer Steve Turner: Jack was present when she and Neal had a furious screaming match in New York, a fight that continued to the bottom of a flight of stairs and culminated with them making frenzied love on the floor. "I think that excited Jack more than making love himself," she averred. "If he had had his choice, I think he would have said that he would rather have watched Neal and me than go to bed with me himself."

left, right two studies of Jack in his early days as a published author. The one on the right was the official publicity shot used by Harcourt Brace for *The Town and the City*. Note the complete absence of beret and bongos – beatniks were something else, as Jack would later try to explain.

After Jack phoned Neal to beg for a place to stay, LuAnne was left to devise a way of getting back to Denver when Neal arrived to take him from the Blackstone to the Liberty Street apartment Carolyn had rented while her husband was a'roaming. Although delighted to see Carolyn again, Jack stayed only a few days, spending his nights cruising the Fillmore area jazz clubs with Neal, sometimes crossing the bay to Richmond, which boasted some good musical hang-outs of its own.

It was here that he first heard and became a fan of the Cuban-born jazz singer, Slim Gaillard. A truly hip and unique creature, Gaillard also played a number of instruments and danced. But his most distinctive talent lay in his creation of a word-play form called "vout," in which the bonuses of "avouti" or "orooni" were added to the end of words in surreal fashion. Thus, Jack would write in *On the Road* that Gaillard's world was "just one big orooni."

His journey back to New York (when Gabrielle had again telegraphed him his bus fare) saw Jack take the scenic route via Washington State, Idaho, Montana and Michigan—another great swathe of the country he could add to his list of "been there, dug that"s—and enabled him to call on Edie, still his wife, in Grosse Point before moving on to Ozone Park and Gabrielle's smothering love. Six weeks after his return, on March 29, Jack learned that

above Powell Street, San Francisco in the mid-1940s.

above left would you leave your car with this man if you knew his juvenile record? Neal Cassady at work as a parking lot attendant.

left snapshot of a sixteen-year-old LuAnne Henderson strutting her stuff.

he was to be a published author at last—Harcourt Brace had decided to go with *The Town and The City*, but only after Jack had carried out some revisions with his editor, Robert Giroux. The company was prepared to offer him an advance of $1,000. Not a fortune, and not enough to buy a Californian ranch, but enough to repay some of Mémère's past generosity.

Even as he wrote excitedly to Neal, Jack knew he also owed a great debt to Mark van Doren, his and Allen Ginsberg's old Columbia teacher. When Scribner's rejected the novel, Ginsberg had taken it to the Pulitzer Prize-winning academic who, after meeting Jack, had passed it on to Giroux with a note full of complimentary remarks. Author and editor set to work on what would prove a lengthy process made more arduous by the fact that Jack devoted his nights to work on *On the Road*, at this stage an allegorical fable in which the hero (Jack? Neal?) underwent a series of trials before he reached a state of repentant purity.

May saw Jack's boot-heels headed west once more, but he found Denver empty of his old friends. As he described it in *On the Road*, it was there and then that he had an intense "satori"—the word Zen Buddhists use to describe a revelatory flash of perception. Down and depressed, he found himself identifying with the poor blacks he saw in the city's so-called

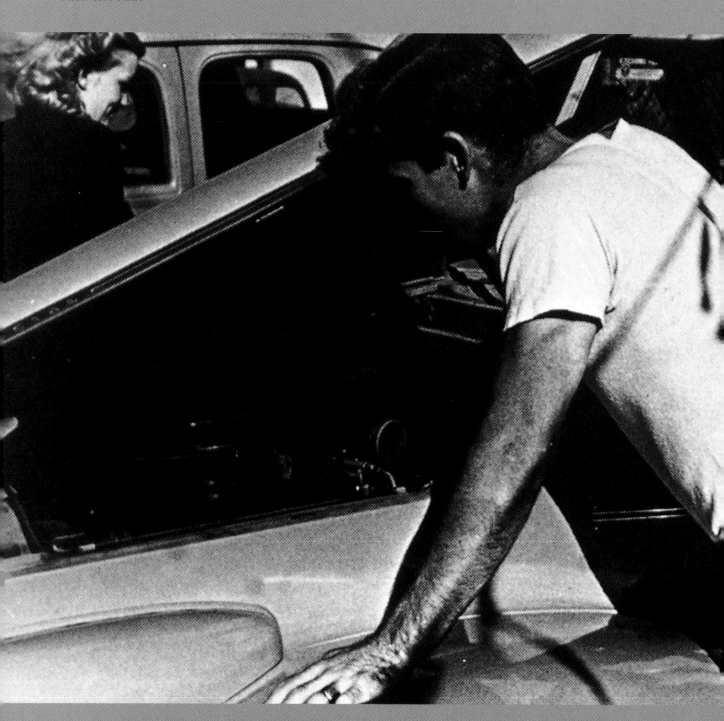

"colored" section and longed that he, too, was black and could share what he perceived as their vivacity, their spirituality, sense of self and their soulful music. Like many of the Beats, Jack would articulate and adopt this romantic (and frankly patronising) ideal, best described by Norman Mailer in *The White Negro*, his celebrated 1957 essay on the hipsters.

Next stop San Francisco and the ever-welcoming smiles of Neal and Carolyn, now ensconced in another new home, on Russian Hill. Jack and Neal picked up just where they had left off, goofing around town and having a fine old rambunctious time while Carolyn stayed home with little Cathleen, ignored and increasingly fed up. Her growing resentment flared into an understandable fit of rage one morning when they sloped in after another night on the tiles and she ordered them out of the house, not knowing what else to do. **"We both regretted it later,"** she told Steve Turner, **"and it took me a long time to realize that sending people away doesn't solve anything."**

Maybe not, but it can often provide a vital, much-needed kick in the pants. Which is what it gave Jack and Neal. After a couple more days as life-and-soul-of-the-party animals, they headed for Denver where Neal, inspired by a marijuana-induced vision that he should get together with his long-lost father, took Jack on another quest through the depressing hell that had once been his world. But there was no sign of him, or anyone who knew if he was alive, dead or just out on the road somewhere.

Which is where they themselves headed, courtesy of a local car dealer looking for someone to deliver a 1947 Cadillac limo to a client in Chicago. Offering a heart-felt prayer of thanks to St. Christopher, Neal clambered behind the wheel and tore out of the parking lot towards Route 6. According to Jack's graphic record of that particular trip,

Neal maintained a steady 110 mph on the long straight stretches of highway, only reducing his speed to a modest 80 mph for bends. The radio pumped, Neal laughed, gibbered and beat time on the dash, and they reached Chicago in what probably still stands as record time.

above left Neal looks over the engine of a possible acquisition in 1947 while Carolyn (in background) checks out the alternatives on offer.

Diving into the fun and games on offer in Chicago's notorious Loop district, where Jack was particularly impressed by the playing of George Shearing, the blind British jazz pianist, he and Neal boarded a bus for Grosse Point and another reunion with Edie. She fixed it for them to stay at the family home of Virginia Tyson, one of her friends. Virginia's parents were in Nova Scotia, so the duo had the run of a spread with four bedrooms (each with its own bathroom), a maid who fetched, carried and cooked for them (candle-lit dinners a speciality) and a grand piano on which Jack doodled to accompany his scat-singing.

They enjoyed a week of country club mingling with Edie, Virginia and their friends, their stay enabling Jack and Edie to talk seriously and at length about their relationship, such as it was. By the time he and Neal departed for

New York—and the new house Gabrielle had rented in Richmond Hill, Queens—Jack had arranged an amicable agreement for his marriage to be annulled and a Parker family lawyer began drawing up the formal paperwork. The last lap of their epic journey was as passengers in a Chrysler that was being delivered to New York, which gave Neal a break from driving duties and the two men a chance to reaffirm their friendship.

After a brief stay at Richmond Hill, Neal headed off to begin a long affair with Diana Hansen, a model he had met at a party. He would still be with Diana on January 26, 1950, when Carolyn gave birth to their second daughter, Jamie, in San Francisco. Jack, meanwhile, was busy transferring a headful of vivid memories to the tips of his fingers and through the keys of his trusty typewriter to the growing stack of pages that made up the latest episodes of *On the Road*.

All in all, the reviews for *The Town and the City* were pretty positive when it was published in March, 1950—with one noted exception.

While the *The New York Times* considered that it contained a laudable depth of vision, *The Lowell Sun* saw only weakly drawn characters fixated on booze, sex and drugs and a tendency to use "vulgar" language, although its editor did run a piece when Jack came home to star at a signing party, the guest list for which included a posse of supportive hometown buddies.

More recent buddies were equally supportive. Justin Brierly wrote an article for *The Denver Post* and set up a book-signing session in a local department store, while Alan Temko published a glowing review in *The Rocky Mountain Herald*. After only a few weeks, however, Harcourt Brace responded to poor sales figures by pulling their advertising budget. Jack's balloon of hope deflated.

In late May he travelled by bus to Denver once more to carry out the signing session arranged by Justin Brierly, staying with Ed White and hitting the city's clubs and bars with him, Al Hinkle and Frank Jefferies.

Neal was back in town, too, and planning a trip to Mexico where he aimed to get a quickie divorce from Carolyn. Diana Hansen was now five months pregnant and wanted Neal to do the right thing by her, even if it meant doing wrong by Carolyn, with whom he remained madly in love. With no real plans of his own, Jack needed no arm-twisting to join Neal and Frank Jefferies when they embarked on their journey towards Mexico City, where Bill and Joan Burroughs now resided.

Down through the rocky moonscapes of New Mexico they barrelled, across the vast flat plains of West Texas with their surreal eternally nodding oil-pumps and unbroken miles of corn and cotton fields, on to San Antonio with its ghosts of the Alamo, then down Interstate 35 to Laredo and the bridge spanning the dull dun turgid waters of the Rio Grande—the border river most Mexicans call Rio Bravo—into Nuevo Laredo (whose Cadillac Bar is reputed to be the original home of the Singapore Sling cocktail) and on to

2'6

A new novel by

JACK KEROUAC

author of 'The Subterraneans' and
'On the Road'

MAGGIE
CASSIDY

...the vibrant,
demanding,
woman-bodied girl
who fascinated and
confused the man
she yearned
for—a brilliant and
profoundly
moving novel

Monterrey, whose principal radio stations blast "conjunto" music north to chicanos exiled in Texas, before arriving at Ciudad Victoria.

Mexico was a revelation to Jack and Neal, with its foreign tongue only one element of many that combined to make it irresistibly exotic and alluring. The same was true of its dark and beautiful people, who represented nothing so much as the "fellaheen"—the poor and dispossessed—who would one day inherit the world. Captivated by them, Jack was inspired to write: **"They knew who was the father and who was the son of antique life on earth, and made no comment."**

They also made the gauche young men very welcome. In Ciudad Victoria a proferred joint of home-grown grass was accompanied by an offer to take them to where the best action was to be found. After a brief stopover in a whorehouse (shabby couches, a dance floor, mariachi music and only $3.50 for a sweaty wrestle with the girl of your choice), they continued on to Mexico City and the relative peace and calm of a rented apartment next to the house Bill and Joan had called home for the past seven months—partly because Mexico City was a beautiful city of no more than a million souls, partly because drugs were readily available and cheap, and partly because the local police were easily bribed when difficulties arose. Bill was also taking the opportunity to study Mayan history and archaeology.

While Jack settled into a routine of smoking vast quantities of dope, reading the Bible, fighting bouts of dysentery and trying to redefine his style, Frank Jefferies enrolled in an acting course at Mexico City College and Neal headed back to New York alone, buying marijuana with the money Diana Hansen had given him to buy a Mexican divorce.

He married her bigamously on July 10, leaving only an hour later for California, his railroad job in San Luis Obispo and, eventually, his legal wife. Carolyn had reluctantly initiated a divorce suit only after Neal signed a Hansen-composed and typewritten request that she do so, but never received the final papers. Not without serious misgivings, but still in love with her confused man-child husband, Carolyn took him back by year's end. She would not give up on their marriage until 1963.

A few days before Neal made an unhappy woman of Diana, Jack wrote a letter to Ed White that expressed both the inner turmoil he was experiencing and his literary ambitions: "I want to work in revelations, not just spin silly tales for money. I want to fish as deep as possible into my own subconscious in the belief that once that far down, everyone will understand because they are the same that far down."

After taking a short break to vacation at Cape Cod with Lucien Carr and John Clellom Holmes, Jack began the winter season by falling in love. The new object of his affection was Joan Haverty, a tall, sultry dark-haired 20-year-old from Poughkeepsie (Ginsberg cruelly describing her as **"full of a kind of self-effacing naivety, makes dresses as a vocation"**) who had lived with Bill Cannastra—a bisexual "bon viveur" friend of Jack's who threw orgiastic parties—until his death, when he tried to climb out of a

JOAN HAVE

moving subway train window while drunk and was decapitated by a pillar.

Joan had continued to live in Cannastra's loft apartment on 21st Street, and it was there—on November 3—that she and Jack made love for the first time, after a party Lucien Carr threw. No one seems to know why Jack pitched himself into another marriage, nor why he did so with such speed, but Joan became the second Mrs. Kerouac only two weeks later. She would recall that although they had invited only a few close friends to their wedding party, after they were married by a judge in Greenwich Village (Allen Ginsberg was best man while Carr and Holmes acted as witnesses), they found "at least 200 people, almost all of them total strangers" ready to have a high old time.

They were, she said, "a shuffling parade of munchers, guzzlers and sippers . . . by the time the night was over, the floor was covered with cigaret [sic] butts, the beer keg had overflowed, the toilet had been clogged up and a platter of Vienna sausage had fallen behind the refrigerator." Welcome to the Beat Generation, baby! After a brief honeymoon hitching upstate to visit Joan's parents, the newlyweds settled into the 21st Street apartment. While Joan continued to hold down her job at a department store, Jack worked on his revision of *On the Road*. Within weeks, however, he had persuaded his wife that they should move in with Gabrielle in Richmond Hill so that his days would not be spent in lonely isolation.

It was around this time that Jack had his second flash of insight courtesy of Neal Cassady. It came in the form of a massive letter (Jack claimed that it was 40,000 words long, others said closer to 13,000) in Neal's distinctive free-flow narrative style. It included not only graphic accounts of his many and various sexual conquests down the years, but also episodes from his unusual childhood. Only by exploring the past, he told Jack, could one hope to understand the present.

This letter (which Jack compared to James Joyce and Dostoevsky in its impact and power) revived the impressions he'd had when he received Neal's first letter more than two years earlier—he had to write more naturally, and began a series of letters back to Neal that he hoped would help him become, as he put it, **"more interesting and less literary as I go along."**

Not all of these were mailed, but they signalled a weather-change in the way in which Jack Kerouac approached his craft. And that craft would flourish and bloom, like never before, in the coming months.

SUBTERRANEANS

Gabrielle Kerouac gave Jack and Joan's marriage an even chance of success in mid-January 1951 when she decided to get away from the New York cold and stay with Nin in North Carolina. Released from the pressure of her curmudgeonly omnipresence, the two moved into an apartment on West 20th Street, Joan becoming a waitress and Jack taking part-time work as a script reader and synopsis writer at Twentieth Century Fox. Their evenings were spent playing happy families, Jack working at the typewriter and Joan following her vocation as an amateur seamstress.

A cloud obscured Jack's sunshine in March when John Clellon Holmes let him read the manuscript of *Go*. Although relieved to see that Holmes had achieved no more than a workmanlike account of a milieu he had observed maybe too dispassionately—the whole point of the Beats was a passion that Holmes just didn't share—Jack was discomfited by the appearance of long accounts of conversations he'd had with the author. No matter that he had been given the alias "Gene Pasternak" (while Neal became "Hart Kennedy" and Ginsberg was disguised as "David Stofsky"), he felt that something of his soul had been stolen, or at least misappropriated. Then there was that use of his key phrase "Beat Generation."

Now immersed in his quest for the stream-of-consciousness prose he was trying to achieve in the new version of *On the Road*, Jack was frustrated by the inevitable breaks in his near-manic outpourings (inevitably stimulated by benzedrine and gallons of strong coffee) when he had to pause to insert a fresh page in his typewriter.

A brilliant solution came with his use of continuous rolls which were fashioned from 12-feet lengths of drawing paper. The result was a hundred-fold increase in output; he had reached the 34,000-word mark by April 9, and a staggering 86,000 words only 11 days later.

Another time-saving device was to use people's real names rather than waste hours devising pseudonyms for what was, at this stage, a relatively straightforward account of his travels with Neal.

If that were not enough, Jack had also begun work on a separate book he gave the working title *Visions of Neal*, an equally experimental piece that also drew on his *On the Road* notebooks and in which Neal was called "Dean Pomeray." It would be retitled *Visions of Cody* when finally published in 1960, by which time he had already given Neal the name "Cody Pomeray" in *Dharma Bums* and *Book of Dreams*, an alias he would also use in *Big Sur* and *Desolation Angels*, in 1962 and '65 respectively. In the final published version of *On the Road* Neal would, of course, be known as "Dean Moriarty," the inspiration for which name has given rise to much speculation.

Carolyn Cassady, who is better placed than most to pronounce on this matter, is only "pretty certain" that "Cody" owed its origins to William Cody, the Wild West hero (which is how Jack viewed Neal), but admits to having no idea about "Pomeray." Kerouac archivist Dave Moore's theory is that, as early drafts of *On the Road* give Neal the pseudonym Vern Pomeroy [sic], Jack may have been inspired by the real-life Wardell Pomeroy, researcher and co-author of the controversial Kinsey Report (*Sexual Behavior in the Human Male*), who'd quizzed Jack and friends in the mid-1940s.

As for "Dean Moriarty," Carolyn can only think of James Dean for the forename (possible, because Jack didn't settle on his final pseudonyms until after the young actor had died at the wheel of his Porsche Spyder in 1955), and concurs with most opinions by suggesting that "Moriarty" was inspired by Sherlock Holmes' cunning adversary **("Genius, super conman, indestructible, unfathomable—well, you know,"** she says, adding: **"Why didn't I ask him [Jack] more questions? Duh!")**

Jack's second marriage foundered soon after he ceased work on the new draft and his mood swings became more pronounced. (Benzedrine withdrawal, or the natural low that follows a sustained work-driven high? His phlebitis had flared again, in any case, he told Neal.) He began spending more time, including some nights, at Lucien Carr's place, but was pushed to enraged hurt when he returned home one evening to discover Joan in the arms of a work-mate.

While that episode did not break them up, Joan's announcement in June that she was pregnant—and her refusal to have the abortion Jack wanted—was a disagreement too far. Jack moved out to live at Lucien's before settling into Mémère's house in Richmond Hill. Joan, for her part, initiated legal proceedings for pre-natal support while Jack voiced his suspicion to all concerned that the child was not his.

In fact, Jack had already begun an affair of his own, with the artist Adele Morales, before splitting from Joan. Twenty-five years old when she and Jack met, Adele was an archetypal Latin beauty, except for short dark hair where she ought to have had flowing black tresses. She would remain his New York girlfriend for the best part of a year, after which they drifted apart and Adele met and married Norman Mailer. Almost 10 years after they were married, it was Adele that Mailer attempted to stab on the evening he announced his candidacy for the post of New York City's mayor. She survived. Their marriage, naturally, did not.

In July, Jack pitched the draft of *On the Road* to Robert Giroux at Harcourt Brace. He promptly rejected it, so Jack found himself an agent—Rae Everitt at MCA—who sent it to Farrar Strauss & Young. When they suggested it needed a major revision before it could be considered publishable, Jack decided to start over, telling Frank Morley, his editor at British publishers Eyre & Spottiswood, that the book would be "much better" then. He estimated that the re-working would take only two months. This prediction would prove somewhat optimistic.

Jack spent most of August at the Brooklyn VA Hospital having his phlebitis treated, taking the opportunity to write a reminiscing letter to Stella Sampas, back in Lowell. Touching on his hassles with Joan, he concluded: **". . . it'll teach me not to ask a girl to marry me the first night I meet her—and be wary of any quick acceptance of such a crazy proposition. Luckily I have no money . . . and am sick, and she can't make her escapade a profitable one."**

In September Joan got a kind of revenge when Jack was actually arrested and held briefly in jail for non-payment of the $5 weekly contribution he had promised to make to her support.

Returning to his revision of *On the Road* (Ginsberg suggesting an increase in Neal's role and a decrease in the overall length of a book that still had a number of other possible titles, including *Along the Wild Road*, *Souls on the Road* and *Love on the Road*), in late September Jack received news from San Francisco that he had become an "uncle" once more—Neal and Carolyn now had a son, duly named John Allen after Messrs. Kerouac and Ginsberg. Less happily, he heard that Joan Burroughs was dead—tragically shot when Bill had tried to do a drunken "William Tell" act by shooting at a wineglass balanced on her head. The bullet from his pistol hit dead center, but some six inches lower than intended, and Burroughs was still languishing in Mexico City's Lecumbere Prison, awaiting his $2,300 bail, when Joan was buried in the local cemetery.

The call of the West was constant, thanks to Neal's repeated invitations to stay (**"Carolyn will be like your mother,"** he promised ominously) and Henri Cru's suggestion that he could get him work on a ship.

Jack duly arrived in San Francisco on December 18, riding a train south to Los Angeles where crewman Cru was about to arrive on the S.S. President Harding. While he and Jack had a grand reunion, including Christmas Day lunch aboard ship and much drunken revelry in Hollywood and Santa Monica, Cru could not deliver the long-promised berth that could have helped Jack escape Joan's clutches.

He returned to San Francisco and the neat little nest Carolyn had made for him in the attic—a floor mattress, a 6-foot long plywood desk on which to work, a radio and a stack of reading matter. Who could ask for more? He had Neal and Carolyn for company when he wanted, solitude when he

above Neal turns photographer to capture Jack, Carolyn and Cathy Cassady in San Francisco, 1952.

left a wimp no longer, Allen Ginsberg is photographed posing on a New York fire escape in 1953.

85

© STANLEY A. PILTZ   8A-H450

needed it, and the myriad joys of San Francisco on his doorstep when he elected to cut loose.

Which he did, disastrously, on February 8—Neal's birthday—when he went out alone, leaving his friends to celebrate privately. Along the way he picked up a black prostitute and, deciding that Neal should have some of the fun on offer, called home. Neal took the call and told Carolyn that he had to go, Jack was in jail. After he left, Carolyn paced the floor until weariness pushed her into an uneasy sleep. When the two men finally reappeared, very drunk, at dawn's early light, they brought the hooker with them.

Carolyn's demand that the girl be taken somewhere else **("My home was not the place to bring prostitutes—there were children around")** was met by a torrent of abuse from the girl before Jack and Neal scurried off with her. They didn't return home until evening, when a shamefaced Jack retired to his room, only later adding an extra note to the dedication he had written on Carolyn's copy of *The Town and the City.* **"With the deepest apologies I can offer . . . for the fiasco, the foolish Saturday of Neal's birthday, all because I got drunk. Please forgive me, Carolyn. It'll never happen again."**

Eight days after Neal's birthday fiasco, in Albany, New York, Joan Haverty gave birth to a daughter and named her Janet Michelle Kerouac on her birth certificate. Her battle with Jack now became one of establishing his paternity and attempting to extract child support for a daughter he refused to acknowledge.

Not long after, Neal was asked to do a two-week work stint at San Luis Obispo. As he left Carolyn with Jack and the three children, Neal made an ill-considered joke that suggested he was fully aware of the unspoken—and un-acted on—attraction between what he called **"My best pal and my best gal"** when he said: **"Just don't do anything I wouldn't do!"** They didn't. Carolyn was deeply embarrassed, for she was strictly moral when it came to matrimonial fidelity. And Jack was shocked that Neal should have made such a suggestion. Carolyn was a rock, a good and true friend.

More, she was Neal's wife and Neal was his best friend. You didn't do that to your best friend.

right role reversal time as Jack turns cameraman for Neal and Carolyn. She was not, it's obvious, comfortable.

below right Carolyn and Jack with Cathy and Jamie Cassady, in 1952.

So Neal had a frosty reception from Carolyn when he came home. Did he have any idea how hurtful he had been? Did he really suspect they had slept together? Wasn't she worth more to him than the various other women that he had passed on to Jack from time to time? Carolyn was stunned by Neal's response. No, he said, he would not have minded if something had happened between his wife Carolyn and his friend Jack. "Why not?" he added. "It would've been fine."

Angered by Neal's attitude, Carolyn proceeded to break every rule she had ever lived by and determined to call his bluff by seducing Jack. After preparing him a candlelit supper (pizza, salad and wine) once Neal had left

for work and the children were asleep, they made love on the vinyl sofa-bed that stood, permanently open, at the end of the open-plan ground-floor living area, falling asleep in each others arms. As Carolyn has said, in *Off the Road*, when she awoke in the morning " . . . a wave of remorse passed through me. What had I done? I was married to Neal, and now I felt sorry for him as well as afraid of what would happen next." What happened next was a full-blown affair between Carolyn and Jack—never carried out blatantly in front of Neal, which would have been extremely bad form, but as discreetly as possible when he was out or away, and certainly never in front of Cathleen, Jamie or baby John. The effect on the three-way relationship was electrifying. Neal began staying home more, he and Jack circling each other like a pair of prize-fighters in the first round, although their friendship did not appear to suffer. Carolyn was now invited to join "the boys" on evening jaunts to clubs (including a Billie Holiday gig), although she and

Jack took many walks alone to talk, laugh and exchange the little confidences lovers have. This odd situation was never, however, remotely like the arrangement depicted in the 1979 movie *Heart Beat* (based extremely loosely on Carolyn's book of the same name) where a "your turn next" arrangement was shown. **"That would have been horrifying,"** she says firmly.

Jack never wrote about their affair, an uncharacteristic omission Carolyn understands completely. **"People don't realize the times we were living in,"** she said to Steve Turner, and to this writer. **"We were still ruled by Victorian ideals. That's why Jack never wrote about the affair. It just wasn't done. You just didn't write about having sex with your best friend's wife."** Then, tellingly, she added: **"We never admitted it because we were ashamed of it."** Ashamed or not, she found a more considerate, if inhibited, lover in Jack than Neal would ever be. Although she says that Neal needed "a lot of sex," he often did so for self-gratification, without much ceremony. So great was his need for the relief orgasm brought (the ultimate escape hatch, if only for a few moments), he masturbated regularly and openly, even when Carolyn knew or suspected that he was sleeping with her and his second-stringer.

As for Jack and Neal, the added frisson of tension paradoxically created an even stronger bond between them. They spent hours together with Carolyn, declaiming passages from their current reading to each other or recording lengthy stoned conversations on a reel-to-reel tape machine, some of which included contributions from whoever they had dragged home from whatever bar they had been to earlier. All the while Carolyn busied herself with sketching, drawing or painting, she and her work no longer taken for granted.

Ever the observer, Jack would transcribe those tapes laboriously, sometimes using his transcriptions as the opening gambit of the next rap session. Tragically and inevitably, down the years Carolyn managed to save only a few invaluable fragments of the Jack and Neal Shows. One, recorded in San Jose some time in 1952, opens with Neal reading from Proust (Jack correcting his American pronunciation of the name "Gilbert" to make it French) before Jack tears into a section of *Doctor Sax*, slipping hilariously into a WC Fields impression for his narrator voice while Neal punctuates with heartfelt, drawn-out Yeeaaahs. It's vocal jazz, with Jack riffing away blithely, happily to an audience of two obviously dedicated fans, an analogy made truer by his ending the recording with some scat singing of "A Foggy Day In London Town" *à la* Miles Davis' trumpet and a Chet Baker-like vocal rendition of "Funny Valentine." Another tape would survive, in transcripted form, as an extract in *Visions of Cody*.

Thanks to Philip Lamantia, a New York poet who had also moved west, Jack and Neal were introduced to the wonders of peyote, the hallucinogenic drug extracted from cactus and used extensively by ancient native American and South American cultures, a subject on which Lamantia had become something of an expert. Both experienced nausea, though Jack reported having seen "lots of colors."

It was only coincidence that he achieved a breakthrough to greater freedom in his writing around this time, even if he still felt that Neal's essence continued to evade him in the latest version of *On the Road*. Back in New York things had begun to get really interesting. Allen Ginsberg, now

top Neal, Carolyn and son John, in San Jose, 1953.

above Neal and John catch some rays in Los Gatos, 1955.

right Jack and Neal, dressed for winter, in San Jose, 1952.

employed by an advertising agency, had been acting as ad hoc literary agent for Bill Burroughs (whose *Junkie* Jack had also tried to place) and Jack, now that Rae Everitt had left MCA. He succeeded, but only in that he found a home for both with the unlikeliest of publishers—Ace Books, normally an imprint of cheap bodice-ripper romances and private-dick pot-boilers. Confusingly, Ace's interest lay in what they knew as *On the Road* but was, in fact, *Visions of Neal.*

In April the Cassady family left San Francisco to visit Carolyn's family in Nashville, putting themselves out by taking Jack as far as Nogales, New Mexico, where he picked up a bus bound for Mexico City. Bill Burroughs, now at liberty and living in a tiny apartment hardly big enough to accommodate a live-in guest, put up with Jack throughout May and June while he concentrated on building up *Doctor Sax*, the Lowell childhood fantasy he had first drafted in outline four years earlier. Writing to Carolyn, Jack suggested that the Cassadys move to Mexico City, where the living was easy, good and cheap. As Bill Burroughs was paying for everything—food, drugs, drinks and girls—he had Jack down as a cheap freeloader by the time he left Mexico in late June, bound for Nin's home in North Carolina.

In New York during July, Jack learned that Ace were now not sure about his book. Worse, Ginsberg agreed with them, advising Jack to drop or cut some of "the more personal sections." A call to Harcourt Brace warned him that Joan Haverty had also been in touch with them, trying to trace her errant husband. Worse of all, John Clellon Holmes was already at work on a follow-up to *Go*, a novel about a jazz musician—something Jack considered as close to theft as could be, for he'd mused aloud to Holmes about his own vague plans to write a book about the careers of Billie Holiday and Lester Young, notionally entitled *Hold Your Horn High*. His chagrin increased when he learned that Holmes' book was going to be called *The Horn*.

below a pensive Jack and Neal with a similarly engrossed Cathy Cassady.

bottom a portion of *Doctor Sax and The Deception of the Sea Shroud*, a cartoon strip Jack created for the Cassady children in 1953.

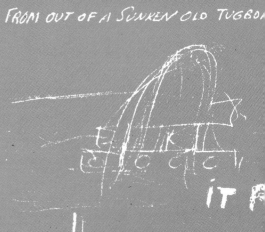

Fleeing New York (and the wrathful Joan), Jack went back to Rocky Mount, then hitch-hiked across country to San Francisco before taking a train to San Jose, where Neal and Carolyn had relocated. Neal found him a job as a brakeman, but Jack hated the joshing he received from his fellow-workers who called him "Caraway" or "caraway-seed" and never achieved the level of confidence or agility Neal had to tackle the task of switching freight cars in motion.

But he did, according to Al Hinkle, like the fact that he got to hang out with the hobos who slept under a bridge at the end of the line, at Watsonville. And he got to resume his love affair with Carolyn. Just as they all seemed to be settling back into the old routine (although Neal was not comfortable with this), Jack packed his things and asked Carolyn to drive him to a seedy Skid Row hotel. While he and Neal had just argued over a pork chop (boys! boys!), Carolyn is certain that Neal's flare-up of jealousy did not represent a serious break in his relationship with Jack.

Living on a diet of cheap fast foods washed down with Coca-Cola or wine, Jack stayed at the Cameo (**"A real poor place . . . it smelled of urine and there were drunks all over the lobby,"** Carolyn recalls) until the railroad laid him off in December. During that period he wrote an impressionistic reflection of the low-life he was deliberately living and the fellaheen surrounding him. It would be published later, in an edition of the *Evergreen Review* magazine, as *October in the Railroad Earth*.

Neal drove Jack back to Mexico City, staying only long enough to score himself a big stash of cheap grass. Still on bail awaiting his trial for Joan's death, Bill Burroughs finally snapped and did a moonlight flit back to the United States, leaving Jack to face the prospect of Christmas alone as a stranger in a strange land, especially as he had received no reply to his letter to Carolyn asking her to come (alone) to Mexico. Flipping a mental coin (which offered him the chance to avoid getting more entangled with Carolyn), he hitch-hiked home to Richmond Hill, spending Christmas and the New Year with Gabrielle as a TV-rapt couch potato, drinking beer . . . and writing the story of his teenage love for Mary Carney. With his now-perfected ability to keep up with the flow of his mind, *Maggie Cassidy* took only three weeks to complete.

Although 1953 dawned with news that Malcolm Cowley – an editorial adviser to Viking Press who could claim friendships with Ernest Hemingway, F. Scott Fitzgerald and William Faulkner – admired Jack's most recent draft of On the Road enough to be proposing it for publication, Jack could not help taking it all with a pinch of salt and a growing sense of frustration.

Although he had been the first to write cogently about the Beat Generation, John Clellon Holmes had beaten him into print. Now, as Burroughs' *Junkie* (its authorship disguised by the alias "William Lee") prepared to give Ace

Books the cause celebre of the 1954 publishing year (and Bill wasn't even a full-time writer, for God's sake!), *On the Road* continued to be rejected. There seemed the very real possibility that he would be among the last to have his words—the True Word—published.

 Down, but surprisingly not out, he hit the road again, regaining his railroad job on the run between San Luis Obispo and San Jose.

Jack moved back into the Cameo Hotel and dangerously experimented with heroin for the "clarity of vision" he said it gave him. He did not inject it, though, he assured a concerned Seymour Wyse; he would, later, rail against hard drugs.

The sea became his brother once more when he was taken on as an officers' saloon waiter on a ship bound for South Korea, then the scene of bitter fighting between U.S.-dominated United Nations forces and the Chinese-backed army of the northern half of that benighted country. Jack only got as far as Mobile, Alabama (via the Panana Canal), when he was found, drunk with a prostitute, when he should have been at work aboard ship. He was ejected from the S.S. William Carruth when it berthed in New Orleans and headed back to Richmond Hill.

Summer brought awareness of the fact that New York—and Greenwich Village especially—had become the focus for a younger generation of so-called "hipsters." It was in that maelstrom of artistic activity that he met and began a fevered affair with Alene Lee, a young petite mixed-race woman who worked for a publishing company specialising in alternative lifestyle and health books. A native New Yorker, she was truly representative of a new-wave clique that Allen Ginsberg had already summarized as "the subterraneans." To Jack, she combined the ideals of African beauty and Western hipness.

Two months into their affair, and spurred on by a massive intake of benzedrine, he spent only 72 hours committing their relationship—including very personal conversations, love letters and frank descriptions of her skills as an enthusiastic lover—to the pages of *The Subterraneans*.

He also included uncharacteristically vague details of a one-night stand he had with novelist-essayist Gore Vidal (given the suitably gorgeous pseudonym Arial Lavalina), which Vidal later said included penetrative intercourse, with Vidal as the dominant partner—something Ginsberg subsequently said Jack would have hated, hence, perhaps, his reluctance to give details. While he was proud of the novel, believing that its radical free-flow styling succeeded in capturing the pace-filled energy of the affair to create a template for "the only possible literature of the future," Alene was stunned and outraged when Jack showed her the manuscript. Not only was it an unforgivable intrusion on her privacy and a betrayal of trust, she was appalled by the notion that such intimacies could find their way into print.

Still, she was sensitive enough to Jack's pride in his work to reject his initial offer to burn the book and settle for the compromise of his changing the location from New York to San Francisco and making her part-Indian, not half-black.

right Alene Lee in conversation with Bill Burroughs in late 1953. The heroine of *The Subterraneans* also helped Burroughs and Allen Ginsberg by typing the collaged manuscripts of their collaborations, *The Yage Letters* and *Queer* during that autumn.

Nevertheless, Alene would spend the rest of her life avoiding all attempts to link her with the character Jack named Mardou Fox, only agreeing to help biographers and essayists who promised, in writing, that they would not reveal her true identity.

Jack's perception of *The Subterraneans* as the real breakthrough in modern literature inspired him to compose a nine-point summary that would be

PANTHER
2/6

JACK KEROUAC

An unashamed
look at their
weird lives...
their wild
loves...in a
jazz-haunted,
desire-
tormented
world

The
Subterraneans

published later as *Essentials of Spontaneous Prose*. One of the few occasions he articulated his theories, it posited that "traditional" literature's fatal weakness lay in a sheep-like observance of outmoded "laws" governing punctuation and revision. These, he suggested, should be replaced by free-association writing that owed no debt to anything but the **"rhythm of rhetorical exhalation and expostulated statement"** and certainly not to any preparation more than focus on the subject, nor to any editing but the changing of real names. Anything more and prose lacked "purity."

Which was pretty rich coming from a man who was still trying, some three years on, to finish rewriting his magnum opus.

Most worrying for many of his friends was Jack's stated belief that drugs were an acceptable form of entry into a world in which an unbroken flow of ideas—not unlike the improvisations of jazz musicians—could be achieved, uncensored by the strictures of a mind fettered by convention. If he saw links between his writing and the wild, unstructured paintings of Jackson Pollock, say, or the bewildering solos being delivered by the likes of jazz giants Charlie Parker and Lester Young, there is evidence to suggest that Jack's recent introduction to Buddhism (courtesy of Allen Ginsberg) also led him to "see" that there could be a meditative quality in artistic spontaneity and there was much to be said for living life—which is, after all, a spontaneous experience—free of energy-sapping expectations or ambition.

Working against that theory, of course, is the fact that Jack Kerouac was, and would remain, a highly competitive animal, capable of hurting when others succeeded and he didn't, and of nursing imagined near-paranoic grudges well past their sell-by date. It would be this fundamental flaw that threw him into the deep angry depression that so marked his later years and transformed him into a misogynist, racist and stumbling drunk who ejected friends and admirers from his house with a stream of verbal filth.

The inevitable break with Alene Lee threw Jack into a despair only lifted by his rediscovery of Henry Thoreau, the Massachussetts-born philosopher-poet and proponent of transcendentalism whose account of a canoeing expedition he undertook up the Concord and Merrimack Rivers in 1839 inspired a desire in Jack to "go back to the woods." That, and his "accidental" discovery of *The Life of Buddha* by Ashvaghosha, the 1st-century Indian poet and mystic who first set out the intricate concepts of Mahayana Buddhism.

Contrary to popular misconception, Jack never subscribed to Zen Buddhism—**"a gentle but goofy form of heresy,"** he called it—but concentrated his studies on translations of Buddhist literature (more Ashvaghosha, in the shape of *The Awakening of Faith in the Mahayana* and *Book of Glory*) and the dense academic works of authors such as Paul Carus (*The Gospel of Buddha*) and Dwight Godard (*A Buddhist Bible*). Much of this early study was undertaken, in early 1954, courtesy of the public library in San Jose, where he moved in February that year.

Mahayana Buddhism offered Jack temporary release from the personal demons implanted in his psyche by the nuns and Jesuit teachers of Lowell, helping him to suppress the dread of death that had so long haunted him.

Buddhism taught him that sensations of alienation and fear of dying came from an ignorant desire founded on a refusal to accept that life is but a dream. Know that and relax your grip through meditation and koans—

above the Mexico City Gang in 1956 – Jack, Allen Ginsberg, Peter and Lafcadio Orlovsky, and Gregory Corso.

right Allen Ginsberg burns the midnight oil.

below right Neal Cassady (right) with two fellow Southern Pacific Railroad conductors, circa 1955.

enigmatic sayings designed to exercize the student's cognitive abilities—and you may that way achieve enlightenment.

Jack would immerse himself in Buddhism for almost 10 years, even abstaining from the "illusion" of sex for long periods, arguing fiercely with Bill Burroughs, who dismissed Buddhism as "psychic junk." He was also intrigued by Neal and Carolyn's conversion to the messages of reincarnation dispensed by the popular medium, Edgar Cayce, and asked them for literature he could give to Nin, who was similarly intrigued. His decision to head for New York followed a minor spat with Neal over their shares of a marijuana stash and his suspicion that Neal had clearly begun to view him— as Burroughs had, in Mexico City—as a freeloader. It is more likely that Neal simply voiced his firmly held opinion that everyone should be able to work.

Early in May, and back in Richmond Hill with Gabrielle, Jack wrote to Ginsberg, mistakenly care of the Cassadys, where Allen had intended to be by this time. He was still in Central America, however, making notes for an ongoing collaboration with Burroughs that would be published as *The Yage Letters*. In that note Jack enthused about Buddhism and grandly offered Ginsberg a copy of the 100-page account he had compiled from his San Jose readings, which would, with later additions Jack made down the years, be collated and published by Viking in 1998 as *Some of the Dharma*.

From that letter we learn that Jack was working hard on two new projects: *San Francisco Blues* (from which he quoted and said he had begun at the

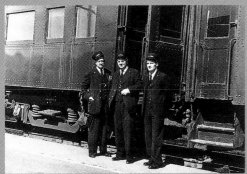

Cameo Hotel "in a rocking chair at the window, looking down on winos and bebop winos and whores and Cop cars") and *Book of Dreams*.

The former was his first stab at writing a full volume of verse, with each poem composed like "a jazz blues chorus" in that it had a formal, pre-set number of "bars," but a content only restricted by what **"spontaneous phrasing and harmonising"** occurred with the beat **"as it waves & waves on by in measured choruses."** *Book of Dreams*, on the other hand, was—as Jack explained in his foreword of same—**"just a collection of dreams that I scribbled after I woke up from my sleep— They were all written spontaneously, nonstop, just like dreams happen, sometimes written before I was even wide awake."** On such writings are entire university courses founded and much tiresome Freudian second-guessing about Jack Kerouac based.

Also in that May letter Jack discussed his ever-present problems with alcohol. "I've been getting sillydrunk [sic] again lately . . . and disgusting myself a la *Subterraneans*," he admitted. **"I want to live a quiet life but I am so weak for booxe booze. I am very unhappy and have nightmares when drinking . . ."** Ginsberg had his own nightmare in August while staying with Carolyn and Neal in San Jose. His infatuation not assuaged, or reciprocated, by the oral sex he performed with Neal down the years, Carolyn was to walk in on them one day, catching them *in flagrante delicto*. She says that her shock was not because the act was homosexual, **"but that someone was intruding on our relationship. It could have been another woman as far as I was concerned . . . [but] Allen had specifically told me that he no longer desired Neal. I had trusted that what he had said was true."**

Ginsberg's eviction from chez Cassady (Carolyn ensuring his departure by driving him to Berkeley and giving him a $20 headstart) led to a transformation in his work and fortune. Moving into a hotel on San Francisco's North Beach he fell in with Sheila Boucher, a hip, beautiful and intelligent 22-year-old with a love of jazz. With Sheila he became part of the literary circle that met every Friday night at the home of poetry guru Kenneth Rexroth to read each other's work. It was there, or at the San Francisco Poetry Center, that he met and befriended local poet Michael McClure and, in turn, the poet-painter-publisher Lawrence Felinghetti who, with arts magazine editor Peter Martin, had opened City Lights the previous year to create the world's first paperback book-store.

San Francisco was jumping, vibrant, alive and Ginsberg immersed himself in the whirl of poetry, music, Oriental philosophies and radical politics in which the city abounded. And it was through painter Robert LaVigne that he met Peter Orlovsky, another aspiring poet freshly discharged from the army and destined to become the most serious long-term partner Allen would ever have. Leaving Sheila Boucher at the Marconi Hotel, he set up house with Orlovsky on Montgomery Street.

Around this time Jack was headed south, back to Mexico City. He had had a frustrating few months since April, when *New World Writing* magazine published an extract from *On the Road*, something Malcolm Cowley had set up to further the chances of his self-imposed task of persuading Viking Press to publish what he considered an important work. Jack's real agent, Sterling

Lord (who had been recommended by Robert Giroux), was having just as hard a time of it, having had rejections from EP Dutton (for *On the Road*), Noonday Press (*Doctor Sax*) and Criterion Press (*The Subterraneans*) and being told by The Philosophical Library that they would only publish Jack's *Wake Up* (his life of the Buddha) if the author personally guaranteed the sale of at least 600 copies. So an escape to Mexico and a period of detachment from the sinful world was just what Jack needed.

Such plans demand a degree of self-control on the part of a disciple, and while Jack initially shunned his usual contacts with hookers, he didn't forego the pleasures of alcohol, marijuana and opium. It was the last two commodities that led him to Esperanza Villanueva, the widow of Dave Tercerero, William Burroughs' former dealer, and Jack fell immediately and hopelessly in love. Hopelessly in more ways than one, for Esperanza was a dying star. Addicted to heroin and living in a slum shack, she earned the money for her drugs by prostitution.

None of that seems to have mattered to Jack who, in *Tristessa*, the novel he would write about their affair, drew comparisons between Esperanza's eyes (like those of the equally doomed Billie Holiday), her "great melancholic voice like Luise Rainer sadfaced Viennese actresses [sic] that made all Ukraine cry in 1910," and her quiet dignified resignation (so like that of the blessed Virgin Mary). It is not difficult to see in Tristessa, the character, a physical representation of the conflict Jack was experiencing between the old Catholic certainties and his new-found opposite and contradictory Buddhist beliefs. One eternally judged and found you wanting, the other said the only sin was to believe that anything was real.

He also continued his investigation of verse, creating a collection of 242 short spontaneous poems (he called them "Choruses"), which he sent to Ginsberg by way of encouragement to follow a similar exploratory route.

They would be published as *Mexico City Blues*.

Allen needed no such stimulus for he had, thanks to Kenneth Rexroth, begun freeing his poetry from traditional strictures. Early in August he had begun work on what would resolve into *Howl*, a magnificent free-form outpouring of epic dimensions that melded everyday idiomatic speech with declamatory Hebrew propheticism, hipster-speak and relentless rhythmic jazz-like riffs to create not only the first major expression of Beat philosophy but explode from the tiny self-contained world of poetry-reading circles and small-circulation magazines into an international "event" riven by controversy. Vilified, impounded and pursued through courts around the world for perceived obscenities, *Howl* made Allen Ginsberg a force to be reckoned with and opened wide the doors of perception to the fact that the Beat movement was a substantial sea-change in artistic expression.

Jack had reservations about *Howl*, pedantically noting those places where Ginsberg had revised the text, so losing all claims to complete spontaneity. He could not, however, fault the poem's power, nor its intrinsic beauty and clarity of message. He arrived in San Francisco early in September to find an excited Allen planning a reading session in a former Fillmore district car repair shop, which would also feature local poets Philip Whalen, Michael McClure, Gary Snyder and Philip Lamantia. He invited Jack and Neal to take part but neither felt confident. In rejecting his offer, they missed out on

below a regular weekend visitor to the E 7th Street apartment Allen Ginsberg and Bill Burroughs shared in late 1953, Jack takes in the sun while Ginsberg takes the shot.

bottom our Man in Guatemala: Allen Ginsberg during his 1953 travels to research the effects of yage, the South American drug extracted from cactus.

Kerouacs wildest tale of love. He says completely new and important things about the real tragedy of narcotics and prostitution.

JACK KEROUAC

TRISTESSA

CONSUL BOOKS

3/6

being part of an historical event at which an audience of only 150 first experienced the overwhelming majestic impact of *Howl*.

On October 13 Jack was a member of a crowd who partook of much local burgundy wine and spurred the readers on with yells of "Go! Go!"—for all the world as if they were at a jazz gig. Allen's reading, like some Hassidic rabbi on speed, left them drained. **"No one had been so outspoken in poetry before,"** recounts Michael McClure. **"We had gone beyond a point of no return—and we were ready for it."** When Jack told Allen that *Howl* was going to make him famous in San Francisco, Kenneth Rexroth stepped in to say it would make him famous "from bridge to bridge," a view echoed next morning in the form of a cable from Lawrence Ferlinghetti, wearing his publisher's hat: **"I greet you at the beginning of a great career. When do I get the manuscript?"**

Within a matter of weeks his City Lights Pocket Poets Series printers began work typesetting the first edition of a book that still remains in print and still sends shivers down the spines of its readers, new and old.

Meeting Gary Snyder and Philip Whalen—both of whom were Buddhists and practised a simple, even monk-like, lifestyle that included periodic stays in the Californian wilderness—gave Jack the chance to discuss his new-found beliefs with people who really knew their subject, even if Whalen followed a Zen path. Late in October Jack eagerly accepted Snyder's invitation to join him and a librarian friend, John Montgomery, as they climbed to the 12,000-foot peak of the Matterhorn in the Sierra Nevada.

While it represented little more than a brisk hike for the San Francisco couple, Jack's more sedentary lifestyle left him exhausted but exhilarated by an expedition he would lovingly describe in *The Dharma Bums*.

That novel paid heartfelt thanks to Snyder's generosity of spirit and his fervent dream of a world in which there was "eternal freedom" for all living creatures, the human beings among which would dedicate their time to praying, hiking and composing spontaneous poetry among the mountains. While keen to adopt Snyder's ideals, and to slough off the last crippling vestiges of his Catholicism, Jack's confusion was obvious enough for the poet to prophesy accurately that Jack Kerouac would end his life "on your deathbed kissing the cross."

Returning to stay with Nin in Rocky Mount for Christmas after a brief stopover with Neal Cassady in Los Gatos, Jack began work on *Visions of Gerard*, his loving, tender and romantic account of his brother's short life and long death. Struggling to reconcile the Buddhist and Catholic portions of his soul, and to come to terms with the suffering Gerard had endured, he succeeded in fusing the core of each doctrine to a beautifully concise **"All is Well, practise Kindness, Heaven is nigh."**

Early in 1956 Jack wrote to the District Rangers headquarters in Washington State, his application to become a fire-warden inspired by Philip Whalen's tales of a stint doing the same job the previous summer in the High Cascades. A positive response, asking him to report for training in June, coincided with the news from Gary Snyder that he planned to leave California on May 5 for two years' study in Japan. Jack made immediate plans to stay with him in his Mill Valley cabin in April before heading for Washington and a week's training.

left Allen Ginsberg: "Jack Kerouac, railroad brakeman's rule-book in his pocket, couch pillows airing on fire-escape three flights up overlooking backyard clotheslines south, my apartment 206 E. 7th Street between Avenues B & C, Lower East Side, Manhattan. Burroughs then in Residence, Corso visited often. Probably September 1953."

Mill Valley was a wonderful experience, giving him time and an idyllic space in which to begin typing *Mexico City Blues* and start work on *Old Angel Midnight*, an experimental project he described to John Clellon Holmes as **"an endless automatic writing piece."** It would languish, unpublished, until 1993.

It also gave him time to benefit from Gary Snyder's superior knowledge of Buddhism during the long walk-talks they took in the evenings. It was at his host's insistence that Jack produced *The Scripture of the Golden Eternity*, a collection of 66 meditations based on the Buddhist concept that all things are essentially different forms of the same thing. **"I call it the golden eternity,"** Jack explained, **"and yet there is no golden eternity because everything is nothing."**

It represented the ultimate paradox.

He would spend six weeks in San Francisco after the three-day party thrown to give Snyder a great send-off, hitch-hiking up the coast to arrive in time for his ranger training and the trek to the immense spooky solitude of the aptly named Desolation Peak, only some 12 miles from the Canadian border. With no alcohol, drugs or sex to divert him, Jack imagined a Shangri-la in which he could meditate, write and maybe glimpse the face of God while he learned the true meaning **"of all this existence and suffering and going to and fro in vain."**

Instead, he found only an all-enveloping loneliness and 63 days and nights of mind-searing boredom (hence the revival of the card game that he and Seymour Wyse had invented so many years before), and his thoughts – rather than considering the infinite questions of life and existence – wandering back to Lowell, to Mary Carney and to what might have been.

SUBTERRANEANS

above George Peppard (as Leo), Leslie Caron (Mardou Fox) and Roddy McDowall (Yuri) in the movie version of *The Subterraneans*. One to avoid!

left the real Leo and Mardou: Jack and Alene Lee pictured by Allen Ginsberg in 1953.

right a drawing of Jack by Carolyn Cassady, 1956.

above Robert Donlon, Neal Cassady, Allen Ginsberg, painter Robert La Vigne and poet Lawrence Ferlinghetti outside Ferlinghetti's City Lights bookstore. Taken by Peter Orlovsky in 1955, when Ginsberg and Ferlinghetti were awaiting the first printed copies of *Howl* from England.

It was seriously negative stuff, prompting him to note despairingly in *Desolation Angels*: "I learned to hate myself because by myself I am only myself . . ." He simply could not function on his own, either spiritually or artistically. John Clellom Holmes had dourly predicted this outcome when Jack announced his plan, but took no satisfaction in being proved right.

After a night on Seattle's tiles, Jack made for a San Francisco abuzz with all things Beat. *Howl* was about to hit the streets, *The New York Times* was publishing a major feature on the 'Frisco poetry scene, and *Life* magazine was preparing features on the likes of Ginsberg, Jack and Gregory Corso, the young, photogenic, ex-jailbird poet Allen had "discovered" in New York back in 1952, since when he'd developed into a formidably precocious talent.

Oddly, for he and his City Lights store and publishing house would reap the harvest of such publicity, Lawrence Ferlinghetti appears to have been annoyed by the attention being given to the scene-stealing Beats. Describing them as "carpetbaggers," he noted that there was already an indigenous San Francisco poetry movement, churlishly dismissing the headline trio as "East Coast people." Swallowing his parochial bile, Ferlinghetti would publish all three in time, and City Light's fortunes did not suffer as a consequence.

D1619
SIGNET
50¢
BOOKS

JACK KEROUAC
ON THE ROAD

This is the
bible of the
"beat generation"
—the explosive bestseller
that tells all about
today's wild youth
and their frenetic search
for Experience and Sensation.

left Lawrence Ferlinghetti (facing camera) and "Shig", manager of the City Lights bookstore, in 1960.

right Neal gets the spiel from a San Francisco used-car salesman, 1955.

below same day – Neal ponders his purchase.

Also publicizing the Beats was Mademoiselle magazine, and it was at the photo session for shots of him and Ginsberg that the most defining picture of Jack was taken, his hair tussled by Corso to add a more "bohemian" air and a silver cross – also Corso's idea – dangling at his throat.

The cross would be cropped out to avoid offending America's non-Christians, but the amended image (Jack looking very healthy from his Desolation Peak sojourn in an open-necked checked work-shirt) would be the one Viking used to grace the jacket of *On the Road* when they published it in the autumn of 1957. Today it graces almost as many T-shirts and posters as the iconographic image of Che Guevara, the ultimate mythic hero.

There can be little doubt that Viking's long-delayed decision to accept Jack's masterpiece was prompted by the wave of publicity that now carried him and the other Beat movement's figureheads to prominence—and thus greater commercial potential.

But credit must also go to the untiring efforts put in by Malcolm Cowley, who had fought Jack's corner long, hard and remorselessly, never accepting the many knock-backs he had endured.

The coincidence of the Beat Generation's rise with that of rock'n'roll, hitherto the most potent articulation of youthful disenchantment and rebellion that was manifesting itself in the form of increased juvenile delinquency, alarmed some of America's most blinkered social commentators.

However, the "rebels" received the full support of one notable academic, Paul Goodman, whose *Growing Up Absurd* (published in 1956) opined that the country's leaders would do well to attend the messages being sent out, especially as many of the older generation were just as "enraged to see earnest and honest effort and humane culture swamped . . . [and are] heartened by the crazy young allies . . ." Jack and Gregory Corso, it is reported, got their first glimpse of Elvis Presley on September 9, 1956, when the new rock sensation made his networked *Ed Sullivan Show* debut and, like millions of others, saw something revelatory and revolutionary in his fusion of white hillbilly music with black rhythm and blues. Corso would admit, though, that they most identified with the infamous "sexual wiggling" of Presley's lithe young trucker's torso, even if Sullivan's camera crew obeyed orders to show Elvis only from waist up on later appearances, lest middle-American matrons be offended. Cropped crucifixes and censored hips? The establishment really was running scared.

There would be much sexual wiggling in Mexico City during the next two months. Jack left New York for the city of fleshly delights in late September, followed in November by Corso, Ginsberg, Peter Orlovsky and Peter's brother, Lafcadio. Before their arrival Jack appears to have devoted most of his time to finishing work on *Tristessa* and to collating his notes for *Desolation Angels*. Once the gang was gathered, though, things deteriorated fast and Jack's Buddhist self-denial went out the window, replaced by the old guilt-riven Catholicism. Drugs were ingested, teenage prostitutes were pursued and hired, and he is reputed to have joined in gay orgies set up by Ginsberg and Orlovsky.

He, Allen and Gregory arrived back in New York to find themselves, if not yet front-page famous, the brightest stars in the Greenwich Village firmament as news of their breakthrough spread. Howl had been published by City Lights in October to anticipated acclaim from expected quarters and numbed outrage from the 'straight' critics who just didn't "get" it.

And Jack was going to be published in the coming year, his years in the wilderness about to end as magazines from around the world began asking him for his views on everything and anything. Even when he had none he gave great quotes.

Fame had finally come for Jack. As time would tell, it had perhaps come too late for Jean-Louis Lebris de Kerouac.

right Jack by Allen. Taken in September 1953 while they were strolling along Tompkins Park, New York.

far right Al Hinkle tries Jack's hat on for size on Russell Street, San Francisco, in 1952.

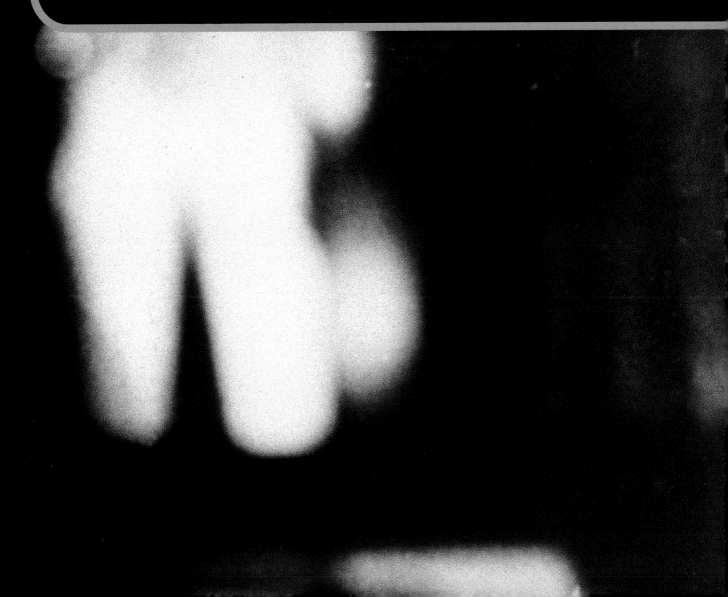

5 1957-1960

LONESOME TRAVELER

TANGIER

Jack's year of glory began inauspiciously with him trapped into long hours of work with Malcolm Cowley on the final draft of On the Road.

As Cowley insisted on what Jack would later describe as "endless revisions" and the insertion of "thousands of needless commas," its creator fretted, powerless to resist his editor's desire (and complete authority) to condense or delete whole segments of text. For his part, Cowley always claimed that Jack was a positive joy to work with and a consummate and keen editor/reviser. Jack also had the tiresome task of securing signed waivers from the real characters featured in the book, so concerned were Viking's legal eagles with the risk of libel actions.

Jack's frustration led to increased drinking and inevitable, often public, confrontations with Cowley and Helen Weaver, his current girlfriend. As time went by his spiritual malaise only increased and he uncharacteristically began missing appointments and challenging people's tolerance with hurtful insults. Blows were exchanged on a number of occasions when fuses proved shorter than he'd expected.

After signing his Viking contract in February Jack purchased a berth on a Yugoslavian ship bound for Tangiers, the Moroccan port in which Burroughs had lived for the last couple of years and which, he promised, offered a hassle-free wealth of cheap drugs and sex. If no greater proof were needed, Bill mentioned that his hotel in the old French quarter—run by a one-time Saigon brothel-keeper—was known to its happy denizens as Villa Delirium.

As Jack quickly learned, Burroughs had somewhat over-gilded the lily and he was soon grumbling that the food was inedible, the opium and hashish of poor quality and the whores overpriced. It became clear that he would not be keeping to his original plan of spending the whole of spring in North Africa before travelling through Europe during the summer months and returning to the U.S. in time for the publication of On the Road.

Before he left Tangiers, however, he did help Burroughs—who was working on *The Naked Lunch*, a novel whose title Jack had suggested—by typing some of the manuscript for him and volunteering constructive criticism.

The arrival in Tangiers of Allen Ginsberg and Peter Orlovsky, in March, came with news that filled Ginsberg with undisguised glee: U.S. Customs had seized 500 copies of *Howl* that had come from London but now formed the basis of an obscenity trial scheduled for a San Francisco court in July. Whatever the outcome of the case, Ginsberg knew full well that the publicity it generated would almost certainly result in the huge sales that usually accompany controversy. It would also, he believed, confirm his status as a leader and principal spokesman of the Beat movement.

Having spent more than six years in the street-wise field of advertising and market research, Ginsberg had a good feel for promotion—no, self-promotion—that Jack Kerouac could never hope to match. Thus, he had ensured that first-edition copies of *Howl* were duly despatched to high-profile figures as disparate as established poets W.H. Auden and T.S. Eliot and the veteran screen idol, Charlie Chaplin. He also invited Marlon Brando, Aldous Huxley and Anaïs Nin to a gala reading at Venice Beach. (Some sources include James Dean on the invitation list, but he was two years dead by then.) Only Nin showed but, as has been observed many times before, she would turn up for the opening of an envelope. Ginsberg ensured coverage of this flop by stripping naked when heckled, ad-libbing grandly: **"The poet always stands naked before the world!"** He was also prepared to give public readings of his works without much prompting, something the innately shy Jack could never do while sober, just as he struggled with TV appearances, press interviews and formal photographic sessions. While both felt—knew—that they were part of something

left while Jack and Peter Orlovsky set to work perfecting their tans on Tangier Beach, Bill Burroughs models his idea of ideal beachwear from the safety of a prone position.

below despite the smile, Jack did not particularly enjoy his stay at Villa Delirium.

below Jack, just before leaving Morocco for Paris in the Spring of 1957.

bottom Montmartre, where Jack communed with the ghosts of the Lost Generation, and the spirits of long departed poets and painters.

right reaping Jack's whirlwind: a 'beatnik' poetry reading in New York, 1959.

important, Ginsberg elected to broadcast the fact (and himself) in huge headlines, while Jack dedicated his artistic energies to creating books that told their story—and proclaimed their message—in more measured tones.

Jack fled Tangiers on April 5, 1957, sailing to the French port of Marseille and making his way to Paris via the ancient Provençal cities of Aix-en-Provence, Arles and Avignon. Gregory Corso was in the French capital, writing *The American Express* for Maurice Girodias' infamous Olympia Press, normally the font of all things pornographic.

Although he spent some time with Corso, and despite the fact that Paris—as ever—was overflowing with artists and writers from all corners of the globe, Jack eschewed such esoteric company and became almost an archetypal American tourist, taking in all the picture postcard sites and wandering through Montmartre, once the haunt of such artistic giants as the painters Toulouse-Lautrec, Utrillo, Braque and Picasso, revolutionary poets like Rimbaud, Apollinaire and Verlaine, and members of Gertrude Stein's Lost Generation, including Hemingway and F. Scott Fitzgerald. He also dived into the old-master riches of the Louvre and other museums and marvelled at ornate architectural glories such as the Paris Opera, Notre-Dame Cathedral and Sacre Coeur.

Maintaining a relentless "If-it's-Tuesday-it-must-be-Brussels" schedule, Jack took a train from Paris to London, listened awe-struck to a performance of Bach's choral masterpiece, "St. Matthew Passion," in the cavernous St. Paul's Cathedral, toured the National Gallery and saw Shakespeare's *Antony and Cleopatra* brought vividly to life on the stage of the Old Vic Theatre. Modern life intruded with his first sight of England's teddy-boys, the sharp-dressed rock'n'roll fans who hung around the Soho district, and the prostitutes who still plied their age-old trade from doorways and curbsides—

though within months the latter would be gone from the streets as British legislators outlawed public soliciting.

Arriving back in New York at month's end, Jack packed Gabrielle up and took her to California, depositing her in a hotel while he spent his time writing at Allen Ginsberg's cottage in Berkeley. It was while in San Francisco that he bumped into LuAnne Henderson, who was struck by how much Kerouac had hardened in the last seven or so years and the fact that he now drank whisky instead of beer. Abandoning his plans to settle in or near San Francisco, after only two months he took Mémêre to Florida, taking a mortgage on a house before leaving for a month's writing in Mexico City.

Returning to New York in readiness for the publication of *On the Road*, Jack fell into an affair with Joyce Glassman, an attractive 21-year-old who would, under her later married name of Johnson, write *Minor Characters*, an aptly titled memoir of that time. She was with Jack during the early hours of September 5 when, acting on a tip-off that *The New York Times* was to publish a review of *On the Road*, he set off to 66th Street and a news vendor who got early editions of Gotham's press.

In the warmth of Donnelly's Bar Jack read the verdict of no lesser an authority than Gilbert Millstein, literary editor of *The Times*.

Describing the publication of *On the Road* as **"a historic occasion, in so far as the exposure of an authentic work of art is of any great moment,"** Millstein went on to say (among many other positive things) that Jack's novel defined the Beat Generation every bit as much as Ernest Hemingway's *The Sun Also Rises* had defined the Lost Generation.

above right lotus-eaters in Tangiers – left to right: Peter Orlovsky, William Burroughs, Allen Ginsberg, Alan Ansen (who was helping type sections of *The Naked Lunch*), Gregory Corso, English electronic music pioneer Ian Sommerville and (seated) novelist Paul Bowles.

below right Tangiers in the late 1940s.

Better still, in Gilbert Millstein's opinion On the Road was simply "the most beautifully executed, the clearest and most important utterance yet made by the generation Kerouac himself named years ago as 'beat,' and whose principal avatar he is."

Even as she read the review with mounting excitement, Joyce could not help but see that Jack appeared puzzled, not happy. With the benefit of 20/20 hindsight, we can perhaps understand some of his feelings that morning, especially considering the long and wearying road he had walked to reach this point. Surely the Millstein review must have made him feel completely vindicated? Only to a point. Remember that Jack had been forced to eke out a hand-to-mouth existence for close to 13 years. His first novel had sunk without trace. Every important publishing figure since then had either screwed with him or told him to get screwed—witness the six completed or near-completed novels collecting dust (*Doctor Sax*, *Maggie Cassidy*, *The Subterraneans*, *Visions of Neal*, *Visions of Gerard* and *Tristessa*) at home or in his agent's files, along with masses of unpublished poetry and short stories. Being told by one man, albeit a very influential one, that your work was worthy of comparison with Hemingway and Thomas Wolfe must have tempted him to stand in the middle of Times Square and yell: **"That's what I've been trying to tell you mothers all along!"**

GREGORY CORSO

He was also cautiously aware that there were many others who would have a say, and he couldn't dare hope that the world of literary criticism was full of Millstein clones. And so it proved, for while there were, undoubtedly, many laurels cast at his feet during the next few weeks, there were also more than a few brickbats hurtled from great heights. While conceding that it was a **"stunning achievement"** in its portrayal of **"a disjointed segment of society,"** David Dempsey told *New York Times Book Review* readers that the characters **"traveled a road that led nowhere"** and was one the author could not afford to travel again.

Time magazine asked a psychiatrist to dissect the character of Dean Moriarty. He concurred with his reviewer colleague's opinion ("a criminal psychotic") to describe him as **"highly emotional, uncooperative, disobedient, stubborn."**

None of this pleased Neal, who was, in any case, unhappy with the way Jack had depicted only the worst, most negative aspects of his character—the very traits he himself hated and was trying to subdue. Not that he would ever

hurt Jack by saying so. But, by portraying Neal as some kind of modern Don Juan, Jack did poor service to a friend who, as Carolyn Cassady has said, **"had no mother-love, ever. This meant that Neal learned to con to survive, and to always be in control and on guard. He hated women, he said, because they were his weakness."** Jack's weakness, according to other reviewers who found *On the Road* resistible, was that he either wrote badly (these included sociologist Paul Goodman, who also loathed his "gratuitous" depiction of anti-social attitudes), or did not deliver a cogent story line, merely strung-together incidents. It was, summarized *The Nation*, nothing more than a "naive paean to madness."

The madness of instant fame would take up the next month of Jack's life as he lurched from one party to another, from one available woman to another (though he continued living with Joyce Glassman), from the clutches of a Broadway producer who wanted him to write a play about the Beat Generation, and the incessant, always flattering requests from magazines for one more feature defining what was hip and what was square, what was cool and what their readers needed to do to be considered both hip and cool.

More importantly, Grove Press had contacted Sterling Lord and a deal had been struck for the publication of *The Subterraneans*—with no cuts or amendments to its explicit text—in 1958, while Viking let him know they would be very pleased if he could make time to discuss the next novel he was going to deliver to them. Getting his head down, his notebooks out and a stack of nasal inhalers stripped and ready, Jack put a huge pot of coffee on the stove and began writing *The Dharma Bums*. He delivered it to Sterling Lord only two weeks later.

Malcolm Cowley once more edited the manuscript, persuading a reluctant Jack to drop an argument with Japhy Ryder (the name alloted to Gary Snyder), which concludes with Ray Smith—Jack's alias—replying to Ryder's pronouncement that he would end his life asking for Catholic rites: **"How did you know, my dear? Didn't you know I was a lay Jesuit?,"** which made Japhy angry with him. In October the long-postponed trial of *Howl* gave Allen Ginsberg his moment in court and the complete vindication of City Lights when it was finally ruled that he had not written, and Lawrence Ferlinghetti had not published, an obscene book. Making his first TV appearance in New York, as John Wingate's guest on WOR-TV's *Nightbeat*, Jack seized his chance to put all the hip "lifestyle" pap into context. Asked exactly what it was he was looking for, he replied: **"I'm waiting for God to show His face."** Jack's aversion to public performances was laid aside most notably in December 1957 when he was persuaded to become the star attraction of a week-long residency at the Village Vanguard, one of New York's most adventurous music venues. The idea of fusing live jazz with poetry was not new (Kenneth Rexroth had long championed the concept, in Chicago during the 1920s and most recently in San Francisco, where the likes of Ferlinghetti and Kenneth Patchen performed with local musicians), and was something Jack's own home-recordings had explored—as had material his old friend Jerry Newman, the record producer, had cut with him in the 1940s. Still uncertain about his own, still unpublished, works, Jack played safe by interspersing poems by Ginsberg and Corso between selections from *Mexico City Blues*.

left a cultural superstar thanks to *Howl*, Allen Ginsberg was soon an alternative A-list celebrity. He is pictured here at an art gallery opening.

top the strain of fame begins to show on Jack in this backstage photo, taken some time in 1959.

above happier times, in 1957, for Ginsberg and Gregory Corso, here being interviewed in Washington Square Park, New York City.

He also performed his gigs supported by the Dutch courage whisky afforded him, and the safety net of a tightly held rosary.

One evening he was accompanied by Steve Allen, who although most famous as a TV talk-show host was also an accomplished jazz pianist. Something clicked between the two, a happy coincidence noted by Bob Thiele, the East Coast A&R director of Dot Records, who suggested that they unite forces for a recording session. Both were thrilled by the idea and, in March 1958, they recorded the album which was released a year later as *Poetry for the Beat Generation* (comprising excerpts from *Mexico City Blues, October in the Railroad Earth* and some unpublished material); a "follow-up" album, *Blues and Haikus,* featured the musical contributions of tenor sax stars Zoot Sims and Al Cohn.

By the time the Steve Allen album was recorded, Jack's fragile ego had been severely fractured by the scathing reviews given *The Subterraneans* when Grove Press rushed it to the book stores in February.

Worst of these was the mauling Jack received from Norman Podhoretz in *Partisan Review.* Basing his feature (chillingly entitled *The Know-Nothing Bohemians*) on his reading of both books, Podhoretz said that neither *On the Road* nor *The Subterraneans* displayed much imagination on the part of an author with a limited vocabulary and an inability to develop his characters.

He also accused Jack of promoting a dangerous anti-intellectualism and sharing with the other Beats a philosophy that preferred incoherence to precision and ignorance to knowledge.

Jack could not even count on the support of Kenneth Rexroth, who, in his review for *The San Francisco Chronicle*, said that while *The Subterraneans* wasn't a bad book, it had **"all the essential ingredients"** of a bad book. Continuing its hate-hate affair with the Beats, *Time* magazine dismissed Jack as **"the latrine laureate of Hobohemia,"** while *New Republic* satisfied its outrage with the simple epithet **"ignorant."**

The comment that most offended Jack, however, was Podhoretz's conclusion that the promotion of passionate primitivism he perceived in Kerouac's work was no different to the delinquency of the **"young savages in leather jackets"** who had emerged as a seemingly dangerous sub-culture during the past few years.

As a man who tried to follow a work-ethic directed by religious awareness, whether Catholic or Buddhist, and who had an intense dislike of the mindless violence depicted in movies like *Rebel Without a Cause* and *The Wild One*, Jack was appalled to find that anyone could make a link between the two. Despite the negative reviews, or maybe because of them, *The Subterraneans* became a best-seller.

Jack began to distance himself as much as possible from the bongo, beret and open-toed sandal brigade now known as "beatniks," thanks to the coining of the mock-derogatory term by *San Francisco Chronicle* columnist Herb Caen in the wake of Russia's successful launching of the satellite, Sputnik-1. That movement had nothing to do with the young men who had careered around America and Mexico in the 1940s in search of the ultimate high and/or the "Secret of Life."

Beatniks were characterized (or justly caricatured) as laid-back black-clad mumblers and bore no relation to the lively, eager crowd that Jack had run with a decade earlier, their enthusiasm matched only by their wide-eyed excitement at the world they discovered on the way, each experience serving as the inspiration for the next.

Unfortunately, it would be comic-strip beatniks who George Peppard (as Jack/Leo Percepied), Leslie Caron (Alene/Mardou Fox) and Roddy McDowall (Corso/Yuri Gilgoric) portrayed when they took the leads in MGM's film version of *The Subterraneans*, which went into production later that year. Distinguished only by a music soundtrack written by Andre Previn and featuring appearances by jazzmen Gerry Mulligan, Art Pepper, Shelley Manne and Art Farmer, it was an unforgivably silly film, although the notion of McDowall playing Gregory Corso is amusing enough to disqualify it from being described as a complete disaster.

Jack cut himself off from such nonsense as much as he could and the only way he knew how—by numbing his senses with alcohol. In March 1958 he

left, right two shots from one of the many photo sessions Jack endured in the late Fifties, following the publication of *On the Road* in 1957.

and Mémêre moved into a house he bought in Northport, Long Island, where he quickly became a new-born suburbanite, dividing his time between gardening, watching TV and tending to Gabrielle's needs. Money, suddenly, was no problem. Apart from the $15,000 he'd got from MGM for *The Subterraneans*, his bank account now boasted a further $25,000 that an independent company, Tri-way Films, had paid for the right to film *On the Road*. In modern terms those two sums alone equate to more than $300,000. Strangely, Tri-way's was only the first of a number of unsuccessful attempts to transfer *On the Road* to the screen, and although the film rights were reputedly owned for close to 20 years by producer Francis Ford Coppola, it remains (at the time of writing) an unfulfilled dream, despite the existence of a number of scripts drafted by his son, Roman.

Better still, Grove Press had decided to publish *Doctor Sax*, obviously thrilled by the sales success of *The Subterraneans*, while Viking were completely up-beat about *The Dharma Bums*, also destined for the best-seller lists. It certainly did no harm to have two of the country's major publishers fighting for your affections.

Jack's suburban sojourn was disturbed by news from Carolyn that, ironically on Independence Day, July 4, Neal's own independence had been taken from him. He had been sentenced to a draconian two terms of five years to life after being convicted of selling two joints to men who had driven him to work after a party, although he had, in fact, given them the offending items as thanks. They turned out to be undercover narcotics officers. His juvenile record hugely exaggerated by the prosecution and the case heard by a judge who would have sentenced this drug-fiend to death if he'd been allowed, Neal's prison term was to be spent behind the high security walls of San Quentin, whose authorities initially and hurtfully refused to let Jack and Allen's correspondence through. Neal did write to Jack, though, telling him that religion was "the only kick left."

During his imprisonment Neal became a model prisoner, reinvestigated his Catholic roots (even memorizing the names of all the popes in correct chronological order) and won his release, on parole, on June 3, 1960, by which time it had become widely known that he was the folk legend Dean Moriarty, a cross of notoriety he would find both onerous and unbearable.

Meanwhile, back in 1958, Jack's own cross (of unwanted celebrity and rent-a-quote punditry) proved equally tiresome. In November, during a rare public appearance as a panelist in a debate held at the Hunter College Playhouse with the title "Is there a Beat Generation?," an aggressively drunk Jack rounded on fellow debatees Ashley Montagu (who was an eminent anthropologist), *New York Post* editor James Weschler and British novelist Kingsley Amis. Calling them **"a bunch of Communist shits"** who were bent on **"the Sovietization of America,"** he launched into a prepared tirade to explain the etymological links between "Beat," "beatific"

above right Gregory Corso (behind Jack) may be having a good time at this 1959 party, but a despondent (and probably drunk) Kerouac is most definitely not.

far right with Bill Burroughs' cat in Tangiers, 1957

right Jack reflecting – and reflected – in a store window.

and "beatitude" and disclaim any links between Beat lifestyle and the nihilistic violence of teenage hoodlums. This would be published, later, as **"Beatific: The origins of the Beat Generation."**

The following year, 1959, saw Jack apparently happy to vegetate and lubricate himself in Northport, although he did devote time and energy to fine-tuning *Book of Dreams* and to commencing work on a new "road" book, *Lonesome Traveler*. Relationships with Ginsberg had been soured by a bizarre, vitriolic letter Gabrielle had written the previous summer warning Allen and Bill Burroughs **("You miserable bums, all you have in your filthy minds is dirt, sex and dope")** not to mention her son's name in their future "dirty" books. If they did, she said, **"I'll sue you and have you in jail . . . I raised Jack to be decent and I aim to keep him that way." "We don't want sex fiens [sic] or dope fiens [sic] around us . . ."** Jack's mother concluded.

Not even Mémêre's malignant ignorance could stop the main project of early 1959, the production of *Pull My Daisy*, an experimental movie directed by Robert Frank, a photographer Jack had met some time before with Dody Müller, a Swiss-born artist who had also introduced him to the Dutch painter Willem de Kooning, a leading exponent of action painting. Based on the third act of *The Beat Generation*, a play Jack had written in 1957, its action was inspired by the bizarre visit of a progressive bishop to the Cassadys' home in California.

Unable to use the original title (now, incredibly, "owned" by a Hollywood B-movie producer and destined to become a tacky exploitation feature about a beatnik rapist and a raunchy "book of the film" paperback), they settled on *Pull My Daisy*—from an old poem-song by Jack and Allen for which David Amran had composed the melody. Featuring an overdubbed narration by Jack, *Pull My Daisy* starred Gregory Corso, Larry Rivers and Allen Ginsberg.

Never intended to have a greater audience than the one that attended art-house cinemas, *Pull My Daisy* would nevertheless be given a gala premiere party in November, in San Francisco, an event hosted by no less a mainstream luminary than the Hollywood star, David Niven. The original script, illustrated by stills from the film production, would be published by Grove Press in 1961.

Jack was in California thanks to a coincidental invitation (and the irresistible offer of $2,000) to appear as a guest on Steve Allen's TV show in Los Angeles, now attracting around 35 million viewers a night. Clad in a sober outfit of grey tweed jacket and grey slacks, Jack seemed ill at ease during the interview segment of his appearance but visibly relaxed when on the safer ground of reading from *On the Road* and *Visions of Cody* while his host tinkled the ivories. It's safe to assume this was the first occasion most of Steve Allen's devoted viewers had been exposed to this form of way-out artistic collaboration. Jack is said to have thrown up when the cameras stopped filming and later had a drunken exchange with Steve Allen, which effectively ended their friendship.

In San Francisco Jack was reunited with Philip Whalen and introduced to fellow poets Lew Welch and Albert Saijo, with whom he enjoyed a number of parties. Welch and Saijo were planning to drive to New York and he readily accepted their offer of a lift home. During that trip they composed a

right a British paperback copy of *Lonesome Traveler*. Note the amended spelling of the title and the price – about 12p in decimalised money!

PAN
books G6

LONESOME TRAVELLER
Jack Kerouac

The Los Angeles
waterfront,
Mexico, New York,
Morocco, Paris,
London . . .
as seen by the
same uninhibited,
rebellious eye
that made
ON THE ROAD
a sensational
bestseller

2/6

left, right compare and contrast . . . Jack and Gregory
Corso pictured during the same poetry reading in 1959.
The despair and growing unhappiness of Jack's life is
clear to see as he nurses a beer, while Corso reads his
work to a rapt audience.

number of haiku together. In 1998, the verses Saijo, Welch and Jack created were published as *Trip Trap: Haiku on the Road*.

Oddly, he made no effort to contact Carolyn Cassady while in California, despite being fully aware of her parlous financial state and the emotional turmoil she was suffering during Neal's continued incarceration. It was, sadly, typical of the cold way Jack had begun to treat old friends and lovers, and no one can condone that. Except the ever-gracious Carolyn, who holds to her trust in Jack's later confession that he could not bear the thought of her seeing him in such a sorry physical and psychological state. What others perceive as cruelty she prefers to consider a manifestation of his weakness.

All in all, 1959 had not been a distinguished year for Jack. His drinking had grown worse—the few visitors Gabrielle allowed in the house reported the consumption of a quart of whisky a day by an increasingly bloated and surly King of the Beats who now indulged in sneering, foul-mouthed exchanges with his equally vicious-tongued mother. He had, it's true, involved himself in friendly discussion encounters with radical, free-thinking Catholic academics and was able to contribute some poems to *Jubilee*, a Catholic magazine. And poet Howard Hart found in him a lively participant in exchanges they shared about art criticism and European Catholicism. But he was in a distinct minority.

Jack and Mémêre also moved again, this time to a new house on Earl Avenue, Northport. They had planned to go to Florida in the summer but matrimonial problems between Nin and Paul Blake forced Gabrielle's premature return from Rocky Mount and a new home seemed a better alternative than a holiday in the sun.

As Jack's alcohol intake increased and his presence at New York soires decreased, people could be forgiven for believing that Jack had contributed as much as he ever would, either as creative writer or human being. He had been just about everywhere he wanted before the publication of On the Road, and there were few signs that anything worthwhile was resulting from his existence since.

above left another night, another bar. Jack finding the same refuge as his father, Leo.

far left a famous drunk is still a drunk. Ask any girl.

left where's the booze . . . ?

They were, tragically, to be proved right in most respects.

6 1960-1969

DESOLATION ANGEL

While the Kerouac publishing bandwagon rolled on, resulting in the publication in 1960 of no fewer than five more books—*Lonesome Traveler*, *Book of Dreams*, *Tristessa*, *Visions of Cody* and *Scripture of the Golden Eternity*—their author continued to fall into the physical and spiritual declines from which he would occasionally rally but which would eventually drive him into a self-imposed reclusion from the increasing madness that fame, or notoriety, had brought to his life.

Besides the negative frustration that his talents had been recognized so belatedly, he had to live with the even greater volume of criticism that poured scorn on his more challenging literary works. *Doctor Sax* and *Maggie Cassidy*, both of which were published in 1959, had been severely dealt with by most reviewers.

Jack took such criticism hard, for he had never in any respect been thick-skinned. Every unfavourable review he took as a personal attack. He simply responded in kind, with verbal onslaughts that were usually as ill-considered as they were virulent.

He was only too aware that many of those who now sought his company did so sycophantically, fulfilling their own sad need to be seen with someone famous. Like so many people who make the leap from obscurity to fame, Jack often had difficulty in establishing who was genuinely interested in him and who was a star-struck groupie. Unfortunately, he also believed that some old friends were freeloading on his money or hospitality and pushed many such people's patience well past the limit by freezing them out.

Such anguish was most easily anaesthetized with drink and he endured the inevitable repercussions of spending his days in a whisky daze: in April he fell heavily in New York's Penn Station, smashing his elbow in the process; in May another fall, in the Bowery, resulted in bad cuts to his face and scalp. It couldn't continue like this for long.

Lawrence Ferlinghetti came to the rescue in April, when he invited Jack to San Francisco where he could complete revision work on *Book of Dreams*. City Lights planned to publish the results of Jack's dream-notes, begun in 1952 and to which he had returned, off and on, during the intervening years. Ferlinghetti offered him the use of a cabin he owned in Bixby Canyon, by the Pacific Ocean shore, and part of the rocky gorge known as Big Sur. Completely private, it should have afforded the solitude he needed to work.

Jack readily agreed, subject to Ferlinghetti promising not to tell anyone— not even old friends—that he was in town. More than anything, he did not want to run the risk of fans, college students or reporters hassling him. In mid-July he caught a train for San Francisco and blew his own best-laid plans by making straight for the Vesuvio Caf on North Beach, one of the most popular and least low-profile Beat haunts. After a few drinks he headed for City Lights and set off on a two-day marathon of bar-hopping guaranteed to broadcast his arrival to anyone who cared.

right immortalized with a San Francisco street named for him, Jack Kerouac's image nestles alongside the City Lights store in North Beach.

above Jack reads his work on *The Steve Allen Show* in November 1959. Supported on this occasion by his host's piano-playing, Jack threw up when filming stopped and later rowed with Allen.

right digging some sounds. No matter what his mood or condition, Jack always had music playing somewhere in the house.

far right Lawrence Ferlinghetti's country cabin in Bixby Canyon, Big Sur.

He reached Bixby Canyon by taking a bus to Monterey and cab from there, arriving after nightfall. His first two weeks at Big Sur were just what the doctor ordered. He hiked through the magnificent wilderness, cut wood to fuel the stove on which he cooked his meals, and read Robert Louis Stevenson's classic horror-tale *Dr. Jekyll and Mr. Hyde*. If the spirit of Doctor Sax was abroad, he didn't visit Big Sur while Jack was there, but it was a strange choice of reading for nights when the sea-fog crept in under the cabin door, the trees rustled with unexpected noises and the sound of waves boomed up the ravine. Entranced by their incessant resonation, he spent hours on the foreshore trying to translate them into the phonetics he would use when he wrote *Big Sur*, his remarkable account of that stay.

Jack was alone for long enough to begin experiencing the loneliness and self-doubt that had plagued him on Desolation Peak. He came to the awful conclusion that he had been fooling himself all his life, **"thinking that there was a next thing to do."** Even worse, none of his so-called **"protective devices"** (such as **"thoughts about life or meditations under trees and the 'ultimate' and all that shit"**) offered any respite from the despair he was experiencing and a growing suspicion that he had achieved as much as he ever would.

He hadn't, for *Big Sur* would prove that Jack—whether in the midst of a breakdown or not—could capture and transcribe his experiences with all the consistency and power he had enjoyed 10 years earlier. It is often harrowing reading (for Jack was candid about his own desperate feelings and recognition of his own shortcomings), but *Big Sur* is proof that he still had the ability to conjure magic from a blank page. The problem was that he didn't believe he still could. Add self-pity, self-doubt, a measured steady dose of Mémêre's malice and an indecent amount of alcohol and you have the recipe for disaster and tragedy.

What happened next also had its fair share of farce. Frightened by his inner demons and an overwhelming desire to get drunk and laid, Jack quit Bixby Canyon and headed for the highway. Not too many vehicles had sped by, the drivers of which were studiously ignoring America's most famous hitchhiker, before he realized that his hitching days were over. He had walked seven miles under a relentless sun before a pick-up truck stopped to give him a ride into Monterey.

FERLINGHETTI

In San Francisco Jack hit the bars with Philip Whalen and a growing entourage that eventually included Lew Welch, a 17-year-old poet, Paul Smith—who raised the Kerouac hackles by coming on like a moonstruck fan—and a circus roustabout they had picked up along the way. Someone suggested they move the party back to Big Sur for the weekend. On the way Jack, Welch, Smith and the roustabout made a surprise visit to the Cassadys, now living in Los Gatos, some 10 miles south of San Jose.

Carolyn was mortified when her attempt to greet Jack with a kiss was rebuffed by a growling shove, although he would be charm itself the following morning after a mad evening of Italian food and wine bought from a nearby restaurant. Neal, who had found work recapping car tyres in San Jose after being released from prison, was tied up at his job until 2am and they all hit the sack soon after the gang collected him, worn out from his day's exertions.

Carolyn was concerned at Jack's deterioration, and alarmed when he admitted: **"I know now my Buddhism is no help, and why Buddha forbade alcohol . . . but I just can't stop. Thinking of those critics and the rubbish I've gone through with publishers starts filling my mind, and I reach for the bottle . . ."** She was convinced that he knew **"he was being slowly pulled down into the quagmire, and his will was too weak to resist."**

Keen to visit Big Sur, Neal, Carolyn and the children drove there the following weekend, joining a party that had swelled through the day with the arrival of Lawrence Ferlinghetti, Philip Whalen, artist Victor Wong, poet Michael McClure and his wife, Joanna.

The following morning, in the cabin, McClure embarrassed Carolyn by passing round a copy of an erotic poem, Fuck Ode, which he had written for his wife. While Carolyn was discomfited by its liberal use of obscenities and references to things she believed ought to remain between husband and wife, Jack pronounced it **"the most fantastic poem in America."**

That evening, as everyone else joined in a bonfire party on the beach, Jack and Neal sneaked off to buy wine, leaving Carolyn with a soft-singing Paul Smith, who had been coming on to her all day and so incurred Jack's wrath.

Some accounts of that weekend suggest that after joining in a wood-chopping competition and enjoying lunch, Jack collapsed with what he would call **"the final horrors"** of a guilt **"so deep you identify yourself with the devil and God seems far away."** Retiring to the cabin, where he lay pleading to God in French, he was horrified to realize that his collapse, and his every sobbing word, was being observed by Paul Smith. Carolyn (who was, after all, present throughout) has no recollection of any such interlude and believes that this crisis was part of his major collapse later, when he was accompanied by Lew Welch and Jackie Gibson.

When Neal drove back to Los Gatos he took Jack with him in his Jeep, Carolyn and Paul Smith being given a lift in another car. Jack learned that Neal (surprise, surprise) was already involved in a tangled relationship with a woman, Jackie Gibson, who was keen for him to divorce Carolyn and move in with her and Eric, her precocious four-year-old son by the poet Gerd Stern. If Neal hoped that introducing Jack to Jackie would get her off his back, he was spot-on. Within hours of their first meeting the two fell into

right not-So-Merry Prankster: Neal Cassady pictured in 1966 when one of his Merry Prankster party tricks was flipping sledgehammers for hippies who'd come to gawk at the real-life Dean Moriarty.

bed together. Within days Jack had moved in with her, despite the fact that little Eric had the disconcerting habit of wandering in to watch their lovemaking, reputedly beating on Jack's back, furious that he was not the focus of his mother's attention.

When Jackie (who would be renamed Willamine "Billie" Dabney in *Big Sur*) started making noises about the joys of matrimonial bliss, Jack tried to put her off the idea by killing Eric's goldfish with the red wine he poured into their bowl and suggesting she should let him keep a mistress. She was not deterred, so Jack recruited Lew Welch and his girlfriend, Lenore Kandell, for further weekend at Big Sur with Jackie and Eric, engineering another stop-over in Los Gatos where he apparently hoped the subsequent tension or confrontation would shake Jackie off his tail.

In that objective he was doomed to failure. Rather than get into the cat-fight predicted by Lew Welch **("Bring on the saucer of cream!")**, Carolyn and Jackie shared what Carolyn describes as **"an ordinary conversation about children and motherhood."** Jack studiously ignored Jackie and tried to get Carolyn's attention, while Neal seethed alone across the room, apparently furious at his ex-lover's perfidy, even though he had encouraged her affair with Jack! It was a strange and uncomfortable encounter made all the more tragic by the fact that it was the last time that Jack, Neal and Carolyn would be together.

In Bixby Canyon for his last visit to Ferlinghetti's little cabin, Jack made it a memorable night for his companions. Hearing voices in his head, he became convinced that they were plotting to poison him and felt the approach of a nameless evil. Then, as he thought of his mother waiting for him back in Northport and the recent loss of his pet cat, Tyke, he fancied the sound of demons laughing and swore that a bat was flying around.

Just when he thought the horrors could get no worse, Jack experienced a vision of the Virgin Mary, a host of angels and the cross of Christ. As the cross's image faded away he called out: **"I'm with you, Jesus, for always Thank you!"** The next morning Jack asked Lew Welch to drive him back to San Francisco, where he is said to have recounted his vision to Lawrence Ferlinghetti, telling him that he believed God was punishing him for not having accepted Jesus as the true Messiah.

Back in New York Jack became reacquainted with Stanley Twardowicz, a painter he had briefly known in Greenwich Village and who was happy to let Jack watch him work in his studio. Fantasizing about branching out as a painter, a musician or actor, Jack signed up for classes at Lee Strasberg's famous Actor's Studio. And while he got to meet Marlon Brando (who declined the offer of a drink) and Marilyn Monroe (now married to playright Arthur Miller and determined to become a "real" actress), Jack did not even finish his first class. There was to be no Method in his madness after all.

He did, however, write a sad, loving and apologetic letter to Carolyn, hoping she could forgive him for **"that awful night I brought Jackie to your house. So ashamed of that I never came back for my old shirt you'd sewn for me so sweetly . . ."** and that she could **"appreciate the fact that I feel, well, shamed? awful? shitty? for writing about everybody as they are. I always make an effort to clean up the mess by changing names, times, places,** circumstances. **But in years from now no one will see a 'mess' there, just people, just Karma...**" Bad karma.

There was nothing but bad karma one night in January 1961, when Jack, at Allen Ginsberg's insistence, was given a dose of psilocybin—the hallucinogenic extracted from certain Central American mushrooms—by Dr. Timothy Leary. Still a respected Harvard professor who was researching psychedelic drugs, the future bête noire and bogeyman of the Swinging Sixties (who'd soundbite countless thousands of kids to **"tune in, turn on and drop out"** through the doors of perception purportedly opened by LSD), Leary was keen to study the effect of psychedelic drugs on creative artists.

With Ginsberg's help he had already persuaded the likes of poet Robert Lowell, Grove Press publisher Barney Rosset, jazz giants Dizzy Gillespie and Thelonius Monk, as well as painters Willem de Kooning and Franz Kline, to aid his research. Jack was to be next.

It was an experience Dr Leary, who had also been raised in the Catholic faith, would not forget in a hurry. Leary experienced the first bad trip of his life—something to do, in all probability, with the fact that Jack's own trip led him to confront the man from Harvard and shout: "Can your drugs absolve the mortal and venial sins which our beloved saviour, Jesus Christ, the only Son of God, came down and sacrificed his life upon the cross to wash away?" Later, when Ginsberg asked if he had experienced any "greater reality" from the trip, Jack answered succinctly: **"Walking on water wasn't made in a day."** That response encapsulates Jack's later open distaste of the hippie movement and its lazy assumption (largely inspired by the pronouncements of Leary and his acolytes) that enlightenment could be achieved overnight through chemicals. He knew that the path to true spiritual awareness was a long and difficult one studded with the pitfalls and obstacles created by human frailty and ignorance.

That, and what he perceived as their traitorous protests against U.S. involvement in Vietnam (he had always been fiercely patriotic), was enough to inspire Jack to splenetic fury when hippie disciples had the temerity to come calling, unbidden and unwelcome, naively believing that they were about to meet Sal Paradise, the blissed-out narrator of *On the Road.*

Instead, they were confronted by a furious alcoholic who drove them into the night with expletives and oaths.

In April 1961 Jack suffered another bout of phlebitis and Gabrielle suggested that they move from Northport to Orlando, Florida—partly for the sun but mainly to be near Nin and Paul, who were now living there. A house was purchased on Alfred Drive, amid a new tract of suburban housing, only two doors from Jack's sister. After ensuring that Nin was settled in, Jack headed for his last trip to Mexico City to complete work on *Desolation Angels,* his mostly unsatisfactory account of life on Desolation Peak and his travels to Mexico, New York, Tangier and back to Mexico City. It would be a

above One of the legendary typing rolls (this one containing *The Dharma Bums*) that helped Jack create his unbroken stream-of-consciousness narrative style.

left a modern icon checks out examples of religious art.

JACK KEROUAC

THE CLASSIC BEAT NOVEL
BY THE AUTHOR OF <u>ON THE ROAD</u>

BIG SUR

slight and flawed book if only because his one-time gift for superb characterisation had fled, so rendering his descriptions of Ginsberg, Burrough, Corso and Orlovsky (among others) shallow and inconsequential.

There is, of course, the possibility that Jack portrayed them so poorly because he now viewed their lives as having become shallow and inconsequential. He continued to deteriorate as well, fleeing Mexico City when a drug dealer ripped him off. He nevertheless returned to Florida in June with enough benzedrine to give him the 10-day rush required to write *Big Sur*, a last fleeting and tantalizing glimpse of the gifted story-teller who once captured the vivacity and essence of a generation that was unwilling to play by the old rules.

Big Sur is not an "easy" read. A graphic depiction of one's own collapse from alcohol abuse could never be that. But there are many exquisitely observed passages – of Bixby Canyon itself, the precipitous cliffs, the secret coves and caves, and the omnipresent rolling surf, its voice booming through long mist-filled nights when it seemed as if he was the last man on earth. Inevitably, there are ghosts – of the long-dead Gerard, of Tyke the cat and long-lost friendships.

Jack would call it his "most honest" book, but even as he described his painful decline into breakdown and the visions that accompanied his delirium tremens, one is struck by the fact that this honesty did not inspire him to fight his addiction. To celebrate the book's completion he bought himself a case of Cognac. Two weeks later he recovered consciousness in hospital with no knowledge of the time in between. He made for New York and embarked on a four-week binge, running into Bill Burroughs along the way. Burroughs was cold and formal, making it clear that he considered their friendship to be over. Jack drank on to drown his regret.

Early in 1962 Jack found himself in court, not for some drunken outrage but because Joan Haverty had revived her attempts to force him into helping support their daughter, Jan, the 10-year-old he had steadfastly refused to acknowledge. Joan was living in the most abject poverty and saw no reason why her now-famous and prosperous ex-husband should not do the decent thing. On February 20 Jack Kerouac met his daughter for the first time when blood tests were carried out. As before, Ginsberg's brother, Eugene Brooks, was his attorney.

Jan, who died in 1996, aged 44, after a life of addiction, abuse and occasional prostitution, recalled the meeting on a 1987 BBC Radio series, *Rebels*. **"I was unaware [of Joan's paternity suit] at the time and I thought we had some special blood or something that people wanted to know about,"** she told Hugh Sykes. **"He had his own crazy reasons for not admitting that he was my father, mainly that he was afraid of his own emotions ... It was partly because he was busy being a baby himself, I think."**

below Jack with a copy of *The Daily Owl*, the sports and news paper that he used to produce for his boyhood friends in Lowell.

Still denying paternity, despite positive blood tests, Jack was taken aside and persuaded to pay the absolute minimum of child support, a measly $52.68 a month, though he insisted that he was not recognizing Jan herself, only her name. He would never make any effort to help his daughter, even when Allen Ginsberg appraised him of her appalling life on the Lower East Side streets. He was still busy being Gabrielle's baby boy. Jan's genes would out with the publication of three largely autobiographical novels, *Baby Driver*, *Trainsongs* and *Parrot Fever*—the last an account of her mother's death in 1991, which remains unpublished.

Jack began making trips back to Massachusetts, hoping in vain to find the Lowell of his childhood. It had, of course, vanished and his old pals had grown into pillars of the community. George Apostolos—the old G.J. who had once stood in line to share the delights of a New York hooker with Jack and Scotty Beaulieu—was now a respectable insurance agent who had to throw a drunken Jack out of his house when he became too rowdy. And Duke Chiungos, one-time Lowell High football star and bosom buddy, went on record as saying that he didn't think Jack drew a sober breath during the last years of his life.

The sad truth was that Jack was an embarrassment to Lowell, a city that had waved a proud farewell to a shining youth and was now forced to play reluctant host to a bumptious drunk who wrote scurrilous books that important critics said were garbage. When he was invited to appear on a local radio show, in September, he presented Charles Jarvis and James Curtis with the impossible task of controlling a lunatic who babbled, giggled, cried and could barely be understood, his speech was so slurred.

During that particular trip Jack called on Stella Sampas, declaring that he intended to marry her.

Although they had continued writing to each other down the years and Stella was aware of Jack's drink problems, she was appalled by the reality confronting her in the form of an unshaven drunk in a soiled raincoat. She asked her brother, Tony, to take care of him.

At the end of 1962—on Christmas Eve, in fact—Jack and Gabrielle moved into a new house on Long Island and he reconnected with Stanley Twardowicz. "He was an alcoholic by then," recalls the painter. "He wouldn't even eat breakfast before he'd started drinking." Twardowicz also remembers with clarity the occasions when Jack, unable to steer a steady path through the woods that separated their houses, would spend the night where he fell. In the morning, when Mémêre telephoned to ask where Jack was, Twardowicz would follow the trail until he found Jack, still asleep, woke him and helped him home.

Gabrielle's hatred of Allen Ginsberg had not lessened with time. In December 1963, when he and Peter Orlovsky returned to New York from Japan and went to Northport, she refused them entry. To Ginsberg's dismay, Jack made no attempt to over-rule her malevolent diktat.

right bloated and belligerent, Jack plays ungraceful host in Northport, NY, in August 1964 – the same year he and Neal Cassady met for the last time.

far right a faraway look for an unknown photographer back in 1962.

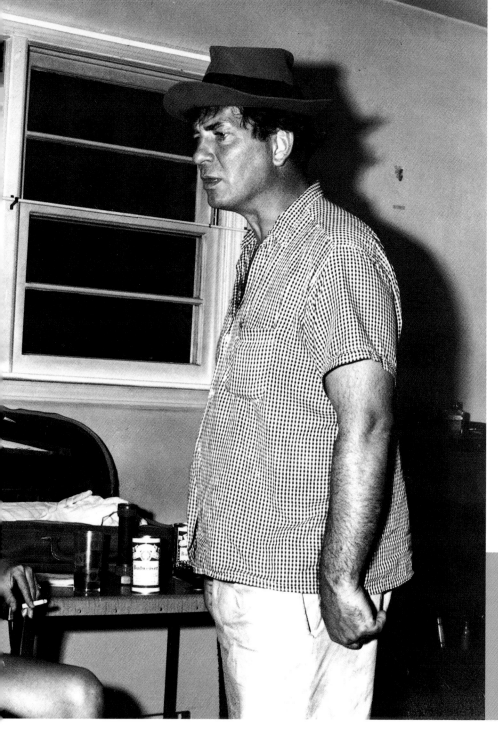

Jack's last-ever meeting with Neal Cassady would not prove any happier. It took place in November 1964, in the unlikely setting of a Park Avenue apartment where members of author Ken Kesey's Merry Pranksters were holed up. A motley collection of acid-freaks, the Pranksters had recruited Neal as a driver and sometime juggler of sledgehammers once he had given up trying to deny his Dean Moriarty image. His renewed craziness forced Carolyn to concede defeat and release him from the family responsibilities and respectability he wanted but could not deliver by divorcing him in 1963, though they would remain close loving friends and Neal would stay a proud loving father who saw more of his children after the divorce.

Kesey's garishly painted bus attracted much attention and comment as it bowled through New York's concrete canyons, its psychedelic artwork reflected by acres of store-window glass. One assumes it caused even greater consternation in sedate Northport, which was where Neal made for once he arrived in the area. And while he and Jack both told Carolyn that their reunion had been joyful, the sparks flying as in days of yore, matters deteriorated rapidly once Jack was introduced to Neal's hippie buddies.

To celebrate Jack's arrival, the Pranksters had draped an American flag over the sofa he was to use. He folded the national emblem up carefully to avoid desecrating it, although he later allowed someone to tie it round his neck. He declined the proffered acid tabs, satisfying himself with the contents of his own bottle of whisky and some of their grass. It was painfully clear that Jack did not, as novelist Robert Stone later recounted, **"see us as angels, seraphs, and all the terrific things that he saw in his own generation . . . Kerouac was eloquent on what jerkabouts we were."** Sal Paradise really was dead even if Dean Moriarty still roared on through the dark American night, slapping out the tempo on the dashboard as a cranked up sound system blasted the beat of a different drum.

Jack and Gabrielle had moved back to Florida (St. Petersburg this time) two months earlier, their move followed, on September 19, by the sudden death of their beloved Nin, who suffered a heart attack. She and Paul Blake had recently separated and her fatal collapse followed a phone call from him asking for a divorce so that he could marry again. Retreating into further drinking, Jack had to face the awful truth that there was now no one to share the responsibility of looking after Mémère, now a hardened drinker herself and always ready to remind him of what a loser he was and how she still missed her little Gerard.

A rare ray of hope glimmered in early 1965 when Grove Press agreed to fund a project Jack had nursed for some time—a trip to France where he intended to trace the Kerouac ancestry in Paris and Brittany. Better still, Evergreen Review was keen to publish three excerpts from the subsequent book before it was published in 1966.

That trip, and Jack's thankfully slender account of it, *Satori in Paris*, is grim testament to how far he had fallen. In Paris the staff of the Bibliothèque National refused access to ancient, invaluable records that the drunk who presented himself to them demanded to see in a language they did not comprehend. Jack would have said it was French, but the gulf between joual and Parisian French proved to be as unbridgeable as it had been when he tried it on Henri Cru. He had no problem communicating with the bartenders and prostitutes who became his boon companions, however, so his second visit to Paris was spent almost entirely in their company.

Abandoning plans to visit the Kerouac homeland in the English county of Cornwall, he made for Britanny and his father's family roots. Somehow or other, another drink with an obliging local always seemed to get in the way of doing any actual research, so when the time came to return to Florida Jack had little more than an extended bar crawl to report. It would take him little more than a week to write his sad account. If Jack came close to a satori, it lay in his realisation that he was not, after all, a Buddhist but **"a Catholic revisiting the ancestral land that fought for Catholicism against impossible odds yet won in the end."** This is no satori. It is merely an overblown and over-romanticized statement of fact. Now doing his anti-social drinking in Tampa, Jack became a bothersome regular at The

above classic Cassady: Neal, where he belonged – behind the wheel of a big car, a pretty girl by his side and some cool sounds on the radio. The girl on this occasion was Ann Murphy.

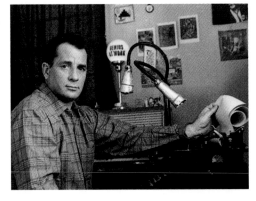

Wild Boar, a bar whose principal clientele were staff and students of the University of Southern Florida. His chief pleasure was to ridicule academics and pick fights with anyone who was unfortunate enough to catch his eye. He also took part in beerbelly-barging contests and suffered an inevitable hernia. He was, in short, the wild boor of The Wild Boar.

March 1966 saw Jack and Garbrielle heading north again, this time to Hyannis, Cape Cod. It was there that Ann Charters found him, her first meeting marked by Gabrielle's whispered suspicion to Jack that she was Jewish (she is, but so what?) and the man whose bibliography she wished to compile making an ugly drunken pass at her. Undeterred, Charters would gain Jack's co-operation and become his posthumous biographer, also securing the task of editing his private letters, the first batch of which (covering the period 1940-1956) would be published by Viking in 1995.

Nothing had prepared Charters for her first sight of Jack, who she later described as looking like **"the battered, lost father of the young Jack in all the dustwrapper photographs."** Although he was only 44 years old, Jack had become Leo, both in appearance and in the darkness that now enveloped his soul and made him utter the same mindless misanthropic bile as Gabrielle, Leo's wife.

He had a break from Mémère, of sorts, that year when his Italian publishers, Arnoldo Montadori, invited him to Rome to celebrate the publication of their 500th book—a translation of *Big Sur*. Jack arrived drunk off the plane and stayed that way all the time he was there, including two doomed attempts to record a TV interview. His translator, Fernanda Pivano, described his appearance on the second occasion as **"very sad, very desperate, defeated, completely defeated."** In Naples he had to be supported when he tried to walk and was jeered off the stage at a public meeting as he defended U.S. action in Vietnam.

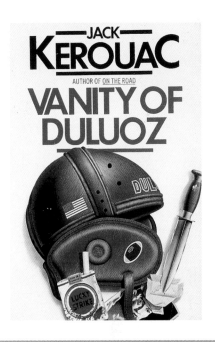

It came as a surprise to everyone, in November that year, when Jack married Stella Sampas in Lowell. Four years older than her groom, Stella had never been married and had never been blessed with the kind of looks that had once attracted her young brother's best friend. A true home-body, she had never left Lowell.

But it was she to whom he wrote when he wanted to keep in touch with his hometown. Shortly after their marriage Jack tried unsuccessfully to buy the house on Beaulieu Avenue in which Gerard had died and, instead, settled on a larger place on Sanders Avenue. Gabrielle moved in with them the day they took over the keys. Still suffering the after effects of a stroke she'd had in Hyannis, she had an able nurse in Stella. Free, too.

In March 1967 Jack returned to work completing *Vanity of Duluoz*, a fresh account of his life around the time he left Lowell for Columbia. If he hoped its completion would explain things to Stella and maybe help recapture the innocence he had lost along the way, his other actions were

far left the house on Sanders Avenue, Lowell, that Jack bought in 1966.

left at home in Northport.

below left the writing on the lamp says it all. . .

guaranteed to leave her bewildered and the rest of Lowell wondering what kind of madman he had become.

At Nicky Sampas's bar Jack began to hold court most nights, getting fall-down drunk and bad-mouthing Stella. Her brothers put up with that, but they drew the line when he brought prostitutes in and Tony Sampas would be forced to eject both him and them. He had friends drive him to other, out-of-town clubs and restaurants, not returning until the early hours, when he would play old jazz records until dawn.

November 1967 brought a surprise visit from Jack's daughter, Jan. Now 15, pregnant and on her way to Mexico with a pony-tailed boyfriend (**"Ha! Genghis Khan!"** Jack is reported to have cried when he first caught sight of him), she had to battle with an episode of *The Beverly Hillbillies* on the TV to carry out a conversation with this stranger, who nevertheless seemed pleased to see her. According to her account, in *Baby Driver,* Jack gave her his blessing to use his name, adding "Yeah, go to Mexico. Write a book." As she left, with her grandmother asking "Is it Caroline? Is it Nin?" from her wheelchair in the corner, Jan felt as if she had been "cheated out of time."

Vanity of Duluoz was published in February 1968, though any celebration was stifled by Jack's receiving word from Carolyn that Neal Cassady had died. It was the second time Carolyn had tried to reach Jack, but Stella had omitted to tell him of the earlier call. Neal's body had been found by the side of railroad track in the Mexican town of San Miguel de Allende on the morning of February 4, dressed only in jeans and a T-shirt—his "uniform" for most of his adventurous life. Another window closed in Jack's soul, though he clung to the belief for some time that it was just another of Neal's goofy pranks. One day he would turn up again, smiling and apologizing . . . but he never did.

Attempting to snap Jack out of his blues, in March Nicky and Tony Sampas bravely took him on a holiday to Spain, Portugal, Switzerland and

right Jack assays a sashay for photographer Lawrence Smith in Northport, 1964.

below a postcard to Smith asking him to use only the face from this picture if his publishers asked for a blow-up.

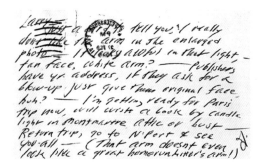

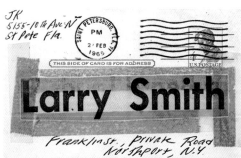

Germany. They might as well have settled for Coney Island, for Jack spent his time getting drunk, smuggling prostitutes into his room, losing his money and collapsing in tears at the slightest excuse.

Allen Ginsberg saw Jack alive for the last time that summer when he was a member of a studio audience for right-wing pundit William Buckley's TV talk-show, *Firing Line*. Jack was a guest with Ed Sanders, leader of the satirical rock group The Fugs, and sociologist Lewis Yablonsky. Drunk and mostly incoherent, Jack only managed to pronounce that the Beat Generation was **"a generation of beatitude, pleasure in life and tenderness"** and saying that, as a Catholic, he believed in **"order,**

tenderness and piety." He also tried to pick an argument with Sanders, asking why he and his kind just "knocked" everything in such a negative fashion. To his credit, Sanders did not rise to the bait. And in an increasingly rare flash of the old Kerouac wit, Jack advised viewers that he had recently been arrested **"for decay."**

The prospect of another winter in a chilly damp Lowell did not thrill Gabrielle and in September Jack was nagged into moving south to Florida once more, this time back to St. Petersburg and a Spanish-style villa. His annual income now less than $10,000, he funded the move by selling his correspondence with Allen Ginsberg to Columbia University's Butler Library.

His creative life during 1969—such as it was—was dedicated to working on *Pic*, a novel he had begun in 1951 but had wisely put aside. Published posthumously in 1971 when the romanticizing of his life began to gain the momentum it would never lose, *Pic* told the tale of Pictorial Review Jackson (really!), a young black North Carolina farmhand.

Archly, and spectacularly unsuccessfully, Jack attempted to represent the nuances of the eponymous narrator's speech patterns **("I watched ever'body all night long, but they was most sleepin' in their chairs and it was too black to see, and I tried to see, but it wasn't no use . . .")** on laborious page after laborious page.

The last interested outsider to meet Jack (there was no phone in his new home) was *Miami Herald* writer Jack McClintock. Sitting in a darkened sitting room graced with Jack's paintings of the Pope and Gerard, and partly sound-tracked by an unwatched television set, McClintock was subjected to a whisky-fuelled tirade against Communists, hippies and the **"Jewish literary mafia."**

Jack also talked about Neal Cassady, blaming Ken Kesey for his old friend's descent and demise, and stressed that he himself was not a beatnik. **"I'm a Catholic,"** he said, thereby suggesting that the two states of mind were mutually exclusive in every way.

On October 20, watching the Galloping Gourmet on TV, Jack was overcome with stomach pains and nausea. In the bathroom he vomited blood. Rushed to St. Anthony's Hospital, he was given 26 blood transfusions but died of what his records described as "haemorrhaging oesophageal varices" the following day. It's fair to assume that a shell-shocked liver also made a substantial contribution.

On October 24, 1969, the body of Jean-Louis Lebris de Kerouac was lowered into its final resting place in Lowell's Edson Roman Catholic Cemetery, after a church service conducted by Father "Spike" Morrisette, the priest who had ministered to the Kerouac family during Jack's childhood and been one of the few to encourage his starry-eyed dreams of becoming a writer and not the insurance man Gabrielle had in mind. Father Spike spoke for them all when he said: "Our hope and our prayer is that Jack has now found complete liberation, sharing our visions of Gerard. Amen. Allelujia."

We are itching to get away from... Portland, Or

top relaxing on Jack Kerouac Street, San Francisco.

left one of the stones from Ben Woitena's memorial sculpture in Lowell.

above Jack Kerouac's grave. He shares it with Stella, who ignored his wishes to be buried with his father and brother in Nashua, New Hampshire.

Among those who stood vigil over Jack's open casket as it rested in the Archambault Funeral Home on Pawtucket Street—across the way from the Stations of the Cross that so fascinated Gerard and terrified the infant ti Jean—were Stella and the Sampas clan, Allen Ginsberg (who would act as a pall-bearer), Gregory Corso (who filmed the interment), John and Shirley Clellon Holmes, Ann Charters and Sterling Lord, Jack's literary agent. No one had thought to invite Carolyn Cassady. Edie Parker was there, though, announcing grandly to a bewildered assembly that she was Mrs. Kerouac. It must have quite upset Stella, but may have been the price she had to pay for ignoring her late husband's oft-stated wish not to be buried in Lowell, but with his father and brother in Nashua, New Hampshire.

It would not be until 1988 that the city of Lowell commemorated its wayward son, with a memorial sculpture in red granite on which are carved quotations from Jack's works. The work of Texan artist Ben Woitena, it stands in a park created when one of Lowell's last surviving mills was demolished, its role long over, its existence a part of a history the vibrant silicon-driven city now consigns to museum displays.

Jack Kerouac is, of course, no museum piece. His works—great, good and bad—remain in print all over the world in scores of languages, his influence on modern literature now acknowledged, his words the subject of university courses, impenetrable theses, seminars and sold-out conferences.

Work continues on the editing of further letters and his personal journals so that a better first-hand account of his life can be read, assuming that work includes no prior agenda-led editing and editorializing. More than that, his works still provide satori for generations who were not yet born when Jack first set out to capture and recount the rebellious spirit of his own times.

And this is the mark of a true artist and a great communicator.

Books by Jack Kerouac

Title	Written	First Published	Publisher
The Sea Is My Brother	1943	Unpublished	
The Town and the City	1946-49	1950	(N.Y.: Harcourt, Brace)
On the Road	1948-56	1957	(N.Y.: Viking)
The Dharma Bums	1957	1958	(Viking
The Subterraneans	1953	1958	(N.Y.: Grove Press)
Doctor Sax	1952	1959	(Grove Press)
Maggie Cassidy	1953	1959	(N.Y.: Avon)
Mexico City Blues	1955	1959	(Grove Press)
Lonesome Traveler	1960	1960	(N.Y.: McGraw-Hill)
Book of Dreams	1952-60	1960	(S.F.: City Lights)
Tristessa	1955-56	1960	(Avon)
Wake Up	1955	Unpublished	
Visions of Cody	1951-52	1960	(N.Y.: New Directions)
The Scripture of the Golden Eternity	1956	1960	(N.Y.:Totem Press)
Pull My Daisy	1959	1961	(Grove Press)
Big Sur	1961	1962	(Grove Press)
Visions of Gerard	1956	1963	(N.Y.: Farrar, Strauss & Giroux)
Desolation Angels	1956, 1961	1965	(N.Y.: Coward, McCann)
Satori in Paris	1965	1966	(Grove Press)
Vanity of Duluoz	1967	1968	(Coward, McCann)
Pic	1951, 1969	1971	(Grove Press)
Scattered Poems	1945-68	1971	(City Lights)
Two Early Stories	1939-40	1973	(N.Y.: Aloe Editions)
Trip Trap: Haiku on the Road	1959	1973	with Albert Saijo and Lew Welch (Bolinas, Ca: Grey Fox Press)
Heaven & Other Poems	1957-62	1977	(Bolinas, Ca: Grey Fox Press)
Pomes All Sizes	1954-65	1992	(City Lights)
Old Angel Midnight	1956	1993	(Grey Fox Press)
Good Blonde & Others	1957-69	1993	(Grey Fox Press)
San Francisco Blues	1954	1995	(N.Y.: Penguin)
Book of Blues	1953-61	1995	(N.Y.: Penguin)
Some of the Dharma	1953-56	1997	(Viking)

Who Was Who

A brief guide to the aliases of principal players in the life and works of Jack Kerouac

Title abbreviations

The Town and the City (T&C); On the Road (OR); Maggie Cassidy (MC); Desolation Angels (DA); The Dharma Bums (DB); The Subterraneans (S); Lonesome Traveler (LT); Doctor Sax (DS); Tristessa (T); Big Sur (BS); Visions of Gerard (VoG); Vanity of Duluoz (VoD); Visions of Cody (VoC); Satori in Paris (SP); Book of Dreams (BoD)

Real name	Fictional alias
Gabrielle Kerouac	Ange (VoD, DS), Marguerite Courbet Martin (T&C), Sal's "Aunt" (OR), Jack's mother
Leo Kerouac	George Martin (T&C), Emil "Pop" Duluoz (VoG, VoD, MC, DS), Jack's father
Caroline Kerouac	Ruth and Elizabeth Martin (T&C), Catherine "Nin" Duluoz (DS), Nin (DB, MC) Jack's sister
Gerard Kerouac	Julian Martin (T&C), Gerard Duluoz (VoG, DS), Jack's brother
George "G.J." Apostolos	Danny "D.J." Mulverhill (T&C), G.J. Rigopoulos (MC, DS), G.J. Rigolopoulos (VoD), Boyhood friend
Aram "Al" Avakian	Chuck Derounian (VoD) Horace Mann, friend
Henry "Scotty" Beaulieu	Scotcho Rouleau (T&C), Paul "Scotty" Boldieu (DS), Scotcho Boldieu (VoD), Boyhood friend
Fred Bertrand	Vinny Bergerac (MC, DS), Boyhood friend
"Happy" Bertrand	Lucky Bergerac (DS)
Leona "Leo" Bertrand	Charlie Bergerac (DS), Parents of Fred
Iris Brodie	Roxanne (S), New York friend
William S. Burroughs (DA, BoD)	Will Dennison (T&C), Wilson Holmes "Will" Hubbard (VoD), Old Bull Lee (OR), Frank Carmody (S), Bull Hubbard Author, friend
Joan Vollmer Burroughs	Jane (OR, S), Mary Dennison (T&C), June (VoD) Wife of above

Mary Carney	Maggie Cassidy (MC, VoD), Mary Gilhooley (T&C) High school sweetheart
Lucien Carr	Kenny Wood (T&C), Damion (OR), Julien Love (BoD, VoC), Sam Vedder (S), Claude de Maubris (VoD)
	Long-time friend
Carolyn Cassady	Camille (OR), Evelyn (VoC, BS, DA, DB), Eleanor (MC)Friend, lover, wife of Neal
Neal Cassady	Dean Moriarty (OR), Cody Pomeray (VoC, DB, DA, BS, BoD), Leroy (S), Friend, muse, inspiration
Billy Chandler	Tommy Campbell (T&C), Dickie Hampshire (DS, VoD), Boyhood friend, killed in WWII
Hal Chase	Chad King (OR), Val Hayes (VoC), Val King (VoC), Friend at Columbia and Denver
Duke Chungas	Bruno Gringas (DS), Telemachus Gringas (VoD), Duke Gringas (VoC), High school football friend
Margaret "Peggy" Coffey	Pauline "Moe" Cole (MC, VoD), High school girlfriend
Gregory Corso	Yuri Gligoric (S), Raphael Urso (DA, BoD), Poet, author
Henri Cru	Remi Boncoeur (OR), Deni Bleu (LT, VD, DA, VoC) Long-time friend in NYC, California
Claude Dahlenburg	Paul (DA), Bud Diefendorf (DB), San Francisco friend
Bob Donlin	Rob Donnelly (DA), an Francisco friend
Robert Duncan	Geoffrey Donald (DA), Poet, author
Allen Eager	Roger Beloit (S), Jazz musician
Lawrence Ferlinghetti	Lorenzo Monsanto (BS), Poet, publisher
Bea Franco	Terry (OR), California girl friend
William Gaddis	Harold Sand (S), Novelist
Bill Garver	Old Bull Gaines (DA, T), Harper (VoC), Friend of William Burroughs
Allen Ginsberg	Leon Levinsky (TC) Irwin Garden (VoD, DA, BS, BoD, VoC), Carlo Marx (OR), Adam Moorad (S), Alvah Goldbook (DB)
Poet, long-time friend, muse	
Louis Ginsberg	Harry Garden (DA), Father of above, also poet
Joyce Glassman	Alyce Newman (DA), Jack's N.Y. girlfriend, biographer (as Joyce Johnson)
Diana Hansen	Inez (OR), Diane (VoC), Neal Cassady's N.Y. wife
Joan Haverty	Laura (OR), Jack's second wife
LuAnne Henderson	Mary Lou (OR), Joanna Dawson (VoC), Annie (S), Cassady's first wife
Al Hinkle	Ed Dunkel (OR), Slim Buckle (VC), Ed Buckle (BoD), Road companion
Helen Hinkle	Galatea Dunkel (OR), Helen Buckle (VoC), Wife of above
Jim Holmes	Tom Snark (OR), Tom Watson (VoC), Friend of Cassady's
John Clellon Holmes	Tom Saybrook (OR), Balliol MacJones (S), James Watson (BoD), Tom Wilson (VoC), Novelist, friend, rival
Herbert Huncke	Junkey (T&C), Elmer Hassel (OR), Huck (BoD, VoC), Early N.Y. friend, author
Natalie Jackson	Rosie Buchanan (DB), Rosemarie (1956 suicide recorded in BoD), Cassady's S.F. girlfriend
Randall Jarrell	Varnum Random (DA)Poet, critic, author
Frank Jeffries	Stan Shephard (OR), Dave Sherman (VoC), Denver friend, road companion
David Kammerer	Waldo Meister (T&C), Franz Mueller (VoD), Dave Stroheim (VoC), Lucien Carr's nemesis
Lenora Kandel	Ramona (BS), Poet, Lew Welch's lover
Bill Keck	Fritz Nicholas (S), Dick Beck (BoD), N.Y. friend
Johnny Koumentzalis	Johnny Kazarakis (MC, VoD), Lowell track star in 1930s
Philip Lamantia	Francis Da Pavia (DB), David D'Angeli (DA), Surrealist poet, magazine editor
Robert Lavigne	Levesque (DA), Robert Browning (BS), S.F. artist, friend of Peter Orlovsky
Alene Lee	Mardou Fox (S), Irene May (BoD), Jack's N.Y. lover, 1953
Lou Little	Lu Libble (MC, VoD), Jack's Columbia football coach
Michael McClure	Ike O'Shay (DB), Patrick McLear (DA, BS), Poet, novelist, dramatist
Norman Mailer	Harvey Marker (DA), Novelist, essayist
Jackie Gibson Mercer	Willamine "Billie" Dabney (BS), S.F. mistress of Cassady, later of Jack's
John Montgomery	Henry Morley (DB), Alex Fairbrother (DA), Poet, author Kerouac West Coast
Robert Morrissette	Jimmy Bisonette (MC), Brother of Caroline Kerouac's first husband, Charlie
Jerry Newman	Larry O'Hara (S), Danny Richman (BOD, VoC), N.Y. record producer
Omar Noël/Jean Fourchette	Ali Zaza (DS), Zouzou (T&C), Zaza Vauriselle (MC), Boyhood friend
Jim O'Dea	Timmy Clancy (MC, VoD), Boyhood friend
Peter Orlovsky	George (DB), Simon Darlovsky (DA, BoD), Poet, Ginsberg's partner
Edie Parker	Judie Smith (T&C), Edna "Johnnie" Palmer (VoD), Elly (VoC), Jack's first wife
Kenneth Rexroth	Reinhold Cacoethes (DB) Poet, essayist
Albert Saijo	George Baso (BS), S.F. friend, road companion
Roland Salvas	Albert "Lousy" Lauzon (MC, DS), Boyhood friend
Charles Sampas	James G Santos (MC), Brother of Sammy and Stella
Sebastian "Sammy" Sampas	Alex Panos (T&C), Sabby Savakis (VoD), Boyhood friend and influence, killed at Anzio, WWII
Stella Sampas	Stavroula Savakis (VoD), Sister of Sammy and Charles, Jack's third wife
Gary Snyder	Japhy Ryder (DB), Jarry Wagner (DA), Gary Snyder (VoD), Poet, essayist, author
Al Sublette	Mal Damlette (BS), Al Damlette (T), S.F. friend
Allan Temko	Roland Major (OR), Irving Minko (BoD), Allen Minko (VoC), Architectural professor, N.Y. friend
Bill Tomson	Roy Johnson (OR), Earl Johnson (VoC), Friend of Cassady, introduced Neal to Carolyn
Gore Vidal	Arial Lavalina (S), Novelist, essayist
Esperanza Villanueva	Tristessa (T), Mexico City prostitute

Alan Watts   Arthur Whane (BS), Alex Aums (DA), Zen Buddhist theologian
Helen Weaver   Ruth Heaper (DA), N.Y. girlfriend
Lew Welch   Dave Wain (BS), Poet, author
Philip Whalen   Warren Coughlin (DB), Ben Fagan (BS), Poet, Zen priest
Ed White   Tim Gray (OR), Guy Green (BOD), Ed Gray (VoC), Columbia friend, architect
William Carlos Williams   Dr Williams (DA), Poet, novelist
Victor Wong   Arthur Ma (BS), S.F. painter, Big Sur, companion
Seymour Wyse   Lionel Smart (VoD, MC, VoC), Horace Mann friend, turned Jack on to modern jazz
Céline Young   Cecily Wayne (VoC, VoD)   Lucien Carr's lover

Selected Bibliography

Amburn, Ellis. Subterranean Kerouac: The Hidden Life of Jack Kerouac, New York, 1998
Cassady, Carolyn. Off the Road. London, 1990
Cassady, Carolyn. Heart Beat: My Life with Jack and Neal. Berkeley, 1976
Charters, Ann. Kerouac: A Biography. London, 1974
Charters, Ann, ed. Selected Letters 1940-1956. New York, 1995
Cook, Bruce. The Beat Generation. New York, 1970
Duberman, Martin. Visions of Kerouac. Boston, 1977
Gifford, Barry & Lee, Lawrence. Jack's Book. London, 1979
Ginsberg, Allen. Visions of The Great Rememberer. Northampton, Mass, 1974
Ginsberg, Allen. Journals, Early Fifties, Early Sixties. New York, 1977
Jarvis, Charles E. Visions of Kerouac. Lowell, Mass, 1973
Johnson, Joyce. Minor Characters . London, 1983
Nicosia, Gerald. Memory Babe: A Critical Biography. New York, 1983
Miles, Barry. Jack Kerouac: King of the Beats. London, 1998
Turner, Steve. Angelheaded Hipster. London, 1996

Acknowledgements

Carolyn Cassady Front Cover, 59, 60, 63, 74 bottom, 86, 92 center, 93 center, 94 top, 107 bottom, /Richard Barry 65, /cartoon by Jack Kerouac 94 bottom, /courtesy of Carolyn Cassady 66 right, 62, 76 top, 91 bottom, 92 top, 101 bottom, 102 bottom, 113 right, 151 top, /photo by Jack Kerouac 91 top, /photo by Neal Cassady 89 center.
Corbis UK Ltd 136-137, 137 right, /Jerry Cooke 64 top, 64 bottom, 76 bottom, /Owen Franken 157 top, /Joseph Schwartz Collection 34-35, 35 right, 80, 81 /Lake County Museum 23, 89 bottom, 93 bottom, /Library Of Congress 16, 39, 66 bottom left, /Morton Beebe-S.F. 139, /The National Archives 75, /Ted Streshinsky 143, /UPI-Bettmann14-15, 15 right, 33, 50 bottom, 77, /UPI 17, 19 bottom, 20 center, 30 left, 56-57, 57 right.
Culver Pictures Inc. Back Endpaper, 73.
From the photographic collection of Dave Moore 140 Top, 157 bottom, /Photographer unknown 22 bottom, 40 bottom right, 46, 47 top, 49 right, 66 left, 97 left, 149 right.
Egmont World Limited /From "Tristessa" by Jack Kerouac 103.
Allen Ginsberg Trust 11, 44, 45, 49 left, 50 top, 88, 97 right, 100 top left, 100-101 center, 102 center, 104, 106, 108, 111 top, 111 bottom, 113 main picture, 116, 117, 118 left, 121 top, 129 right, 129 bottom, /Used with the permission of the Allen Ginsberg Trust 20 bottom, 47 bottom, 51, 55, 74 top.
Globe Photos Inc.1999 /©Jerome Yulsman 126, 127, 134 left.
Harcourt Brace & Company /From "The Town & The City" by Jack Kerouac 53.
HarperCollins Publishers /From "Big Sur" by Jack Kerouac 146, /From "Vanity of Duluoz" by Jack Kerouac 153.
Hulton Getty Picture Collection front arlin, back arlin, 12, 38, 42.
Image Bank /Archive Photos 1, 2-3, 3 right, 5, 8-9, 28 top, 69, 118 bottom right, 121 bottom, /Frank Driggs/Archive Photos 49 center.
©Jerry Bauer 24 top, 25 left, 140 bottom, 144, 145, 147, 152 bottom
Lawrence L. Smith 149 main picture, 152 main Picture, 154, 155.
Magnum Photos /Elliot Erwitt 72, /Burt Glinn 110, 119, 122, 124 Top, 124 bottom, 129 main picture, 132, 133, 134 main picture, 134 bottom.
Reproduced with the permission of Timothy Moran /The Edie Parker Estate 40 Top, /The Henri Cru Estate front endpaper, 114-115, 115 right
Pan Books /From "The Lonesome Traveler" by Jack Kerouac 131.
Panther /From "Maggie Cassidy" by Jack Kerouac 79, /From "The Subterraneans" by Jack Kerouac 98.
Penguin Putnam Inc. /From On The Road by Jack Kerouac. ©1955, 1957 by Jack Kerouac; renewed ©1983 by Stella Kerouac, renewed © by Stella Kerouac and Jan Kerouac. Used with permission of Viking Penguin. a division of Penguin Putnam Inc. 109.
Jeff Prant Postcards 113 top.
Quartet Books Ltd /From "Satori In Paris" by Jack Kerouac 151 bottom right
The Ronald Grant Archive /MGM 84-85, 85 right, 107 top
Steve Turner 19 top, 20 top, 22 top, 82, 152 left, 156, /Courtesy of Judy Machado 27, /Courtesy of Steve Turner 31, 141.

d the city in 1842. It was the eminent English author's
st visit to America and the industrial revolution which
d completely transformed Britain was changing the
e of its former colony in similar fashion. A noted social
ormer, Dickens was keen to see how the new breed of
nerican industrialists were setting about their task and
well, brightest jewel in the American textile-manufac-
ring crown, was as good as a place to start as any.Lying
the junction of the Merrimack and Concord rivers some
miles northwest of Boston, Lowell was established by
ite settlers in 1653 when it was a farming
mmunity known as East Chelmsford. At the beginning
the 19th century the abundance of free water power
m the 35-feet high Pawtucket Falls and the completion
the Middlesex Canal to Boston made the location ideal
entrepreneurs in the cloth and shoe-manufacturing
des. By 1824 the town boasted a network of canals to
rve the mills which lined the Merrimack and two years
er East Chelmsford became an historical footnote
en the now-thriving community was incorporated as a
wn and named for Francis Cabot Lowell, a pioneer tex-
e magnate. Ten years later it achieved the status of
y, sharing with Cambridge the distinction of being co-
at of Middlesex County.Dickens wrote admiringly of
well's clean, wide and tree-lined avenues, so contrast-
g with the mean, narrow, grime-encrusted streets
ich typified Britain's industrial cities. He also
narked warmly about the cheery demeanor and good
portment of the female loom-hands
encountered, and of the two dollars a week they could
rn as workers in this exciting and dynamic new enter-
ise. The harsh truth, however, was that many of those
m-hands were destined for early graves, their lungs
stroyed by the raw lint which flew about their work-
aces, while their homes were mostly ill-built wood-
ame houses which offered no real protection against the
ter col
f long New England winters.During the next 100 years
well continued to grow apace. While it rose to become
e of America's most important industrial sites, earning
elf the nickname 'Spindle City', competition from
eaper imported fabrics and rejuvenated post-Civil War
uthern cotton-growing states began to erode its pros-
rity; mill owners cut wages and workers began to move
ewhere for better-paid employment. And so it was that
well began to welcome large numbers of outsiders who
re ready to take on any work, no matter how poorly
id - immigrants from Greece, Poland, Ireland...and
ench-speaking Quebec, the Canadian province which
y less than 200 miles north and many of whosecitizens
d long since migrated south to live in neighbouring New
mpshire and Vermont.By the end of World War I,
well - now boasting a population of more than 80,000 -
s a cosmopolitan and multicultural city, each immi-
ant group forming its own self-contained community,
eserving its mother-tongue and traditions in homes,
hools, churches, restaurants and clubs, celebrating its
n ages-old anniversaries and festivals, observing its
n social mores to create a sense of continuity and sta-
ity in a world that had grown increasingly unstable,
d nowhere more so than in the employment field.Ten
ars before the first chill blasts of recession signalled
e arrival of the 1930s Depression, Lowell began a
cline every bit as cataclysmic. One by one the cotton
lls were shut down, the surviving few forced (or able)
offer what became breadline paypackets. While the
st of America and the developed world began the
ocess of rebuilding from the ashes of the Great War dur-
g what would be the fun-filled Roaring Twenties,
well's fortunes took a dive. To m
quote Charles Dickens himself, Lowell experienced the
rst of times amid the best of times. Jean-Louis Lebris
Kerouac - the name given on his birth certificate - was
rn into this depressing scenario on March 12, 1922, the
rd child of Joseph Alcide Leo Kirouack (sic) and his
fe, Gabrielle Ange L'Evesque. Their two older children
re Gerard, who was five when his baby brother
rived, and Caroline, a sparky three-year old already
d forever to be known to her family by the pet-name
in'. Jack Kerouac himself was to become known to his

school in Rhode Island. Initially spelling his surname Kérouack, Leo began his w
language newspaper, L'Impartial. His industry and aptitude convinced its own
struggling L'Etoile, charging the young man with the roles of news reporter, adve
tor and typesetter.Leo was 26 years old when he returned to Nashua to court
Quebec, some five miles from the St Lawrence River shore and 60 miles east of t
ancestors from Normandy (Leo's were from Britanny), with the exotica of a hal
when she was an infant, her mother dying tragically young and her father - a mi
from his second wife until his own untimely death in 1909, when Gabrielle was
Gabrielle would return to that job time and again for much of her adult life, even a
than a six-year gap between Leo and Gabrielle's ages to make them badly misma
cy in English enabled him to move gregariously across Lowell's cultural divides
the city district of Pawtucketville, and was most co
mfortable speaking joual, the French-Canadian dialect which would be her son'
education. In fact, Jack would not express himself confidently in English until h
reason than most to call on mother church - and the nuns who ran the local St
Louis de France Parochial School - for spiritual help and sustenance during the
born and undisputed darling, was victim to a succession of illnesses which left h
of rheumatic fever which eventually claimed his life in 1926, when he was onl
Kerouac'
s infancy was spent in a remorseless and unremitting saga of sickbeds, weeping
born out of the holy sisters' conviction that Gerard was a sainted martyr in the
to share. Certainly, Gerard was a devout boy who fervently embraced the church'
er. Too young to comprehend, Jack nevertheless received a mass of powerful im
many spectral sentinels in the grounds of the Franco-American Orphanage on
depicting one of the Stations of the Cross, the twelve stages of brutal horrors inflic
liked to take ti Jean there, talking him through the bestial ordeal in awful detail
heal.e fact is that while Jack Kerouac's best-known and most successful novel, On
best during a relatively brief period of his adulthood, much more of his working
his Lowell childhood, his family and friends.....and the undying memories of the
rest of her life and against whose perfection Jack was forever being compared an
with the publication of Visions of Gerard, a haunting memoir first begun in 1956
of Duluoz' - the fictional name he gave his family in those chronicles.And while Ja
the party line where Gerard was concerned ('the strangest, most angelic gentle c
Cassady, in a 1950 letter), he would forever nurse a guilt-ridden resentment agai
he died, Gerard - enraged when ti Jean disturbed an assemblage he was working
an episode which shocked Jack enough for him to recall it vividly in that same
years earlier in a letter to his sister, Caroline. Then he was undergoing psychoan
ed in a natural childish wish that the perpetrator would die - a wish which had
explained to Nin, 'and ever since, mortified beyond repair, warped in my personal
failing at everything.' The real responsibility for any warping of Jack's personali
beloved Gerard dead she turned the full suffocating weight of her overweaning
slept alongside their mother in the big bed she ought to have shared with her hus
school and dosed with patent medicines. Gabrielle also insisted on supervizing Ja
was a hefty twelve-year old when his mother's bathtime scrubbing caused him t
shame would haunt him for years.While Gabrielle had obviously done her wifely
itself both disgusting and sinful. It was a certitude she would pass on to her son,
got the better of him ('But there's an awful paranoiac element sometimes in orgas
some token venom that splits up in the body,' he'd write in Big Sur) and making hi
term physical relationships.
Gabrielle was also viciously anti-semitic (hadn't 'they' conspired to kill the Lord
week by the rabid Catholic priest, Father Charles Coughlin, on what was one of A
1930s. According to Coughlin, Jewish banking interests had caused the Wall Stre
could be traced either to Jews or those who'd bought into the international Jewis
absorb and retain, even though many of his most trusted and loyal friends in late
The nuns of St Louis de France did their own damage, dinning into Jack the Cath
guilt of Adam's challenge to God by eating the forbidden fruit. And the forbidden
tortured martyrs, graphic examples of the horrible suffering endured by those w
experienced by saints - most especially the young French consumptive, Thérèse
had joined at age 15, was preceded by visions and revelations she dutifully recor
mously published a year or two later.
Thérèse had been canonized in 1925 and became the focus for a cult-like followi
the young French saint as his own patron and inspiration even if later sophisti
lambs, roses and fluffy clouds) dedicated to her glorification. Thérèse's surna
would give that name to the family at the heart of his first published novel, The
Jack transferred to St Joseph's School and the strictures of Jesuit teachers. (
ized them to friend and biographer Charles E Jarvis, adding: 'I wa
Pawtucketville district in 1932. It was only one of a number of reloc
Leo had quit his newspaper job to strike out as a jobbing printer. His
his decline into solace drinking when times grew hard. That, combined
precarious.
Even when he found occasional jobs with better
employers to fire him and make him few real friends.
Convinced that Lowell's city fathers - council officials,
spiracy, Leo published his own newsletter, Spotlight, to rea
cal productions and sports events, including the wrestling
was Leo who filled Jack's head with a convoluted and fancif
ed to Brittany via Wales and Cornwall before settling in Canada.
ly sound (if jumbled), his claims to have recovered memories
were inspired as much by the large quantities of alcohol he was
romanticism and love of the dramatic.